...for a creative, joyful and peaceful... and an authentically expressed voice!

Shahana 4/4/13

YOU ARE MICHELANGELO
...AND YOU ARE DAVID!

AWAKENING THE CREATIVE AND THE CREATION WITHIN

Shahana Dattagupta

ISBN-13: 978-0615772998
ISBN-10: 0615772994
First printing March 27, 2013
Flying Chickadee
PO Box 30021, Seattle, WA 98113-0021
www.flyingchickadee.com

Some essays in this book were first published (in a different form) in the author's online blog *Reflections and Revelations*. See: http://www.reflectionsandrevelations.com

Cover illustration © 2012 Ashok Das
Cover design and interior illustrations by Shahana Dattagupta
Poem *Hiding in the Stone* © 2011 Pallavi Garg
Copy editing and *Chapter Reflections* by Shirin Subhani
Author photograph © 2011 Siddhartha Saha

For

Murali

in gratitude for showing me the best mirror yet,

For

Shirin

in gratitude for creating with me daily,

And for

all those courageous creatives

who open their hearts daily, and chip, chip away to shine forth the Light and Love within...

CONTENTS

PART II: EXERCISING YOUR CREATIVITY

"The best artist has that thought alone
Which is contained within the marble shell;
The sculptor's hand can only break the spell
To free the figures slumbering in the stone."

– Michelangelo

Hiding in the stone

I've heard it said
That figures lie
Hiding in the stone,
For the sculptor to set free

I've often wondered
At this mystery...
How does the sculptor
Know the real story?

I've been fortunate to
Have met many Masters
Adept at their art and
In their own way, unique sculptors

I've felt their glance
Pierce through my soul
Purging everything within
That didn't make me whole

I've experienced
Their words, their music, their art
Set me free, liberate me
To follow my own dear heart
I've let the sands of time
Chisel away
At everything within
That didn't need to stay

I've set upon my path
Seen how my journey
Becomes my destination
When I am present, it's uncanny

I've learned the art
Of looking within
Of trusting life even if
My patience runs thin

I've witnessed how my thoughts
Create my reality
How everything is me
No possibility of duality

Now,
I've given up figuring out
That which is limitless
Un-knowable, inexpressible
Unbounded, formless

I've seen how there's no doing
There can be only being
Loving, Living Life
Laughing, Celebrating,

That the seer, the sight, the scenery
They're all really one
I am the sculptor, I am the chisel,
I am the stone

Pallavi Garg
Seattle, December 18, 2011

INTRODUCTION

CREATIVITY AS HUMAN PURPOSE

"When we consider creativity, we are considering the most elemental and innermost and deeply spiritual aspects of our beings."

– Matthew Fox

"Creativity in the outer arena...is only facilitated by a creative exploration of the inner arena...In the moment that a creative creates, (she) encounters a deeper aspect of the self that I call the quantum self."

– Dr. Amit Goswami

Nearly nine years ago, in the midst of a significant life crisis that included a near-death experience, I jumped off my 'reasonable' and 'constructed' life headlong into my life purpose, even if what exactly that was, was entirely foggy in the moment. I simply surrendered myself to the unseen, the unknown, the uncertain, and began putting one foot in front of the other.

The unexpected synergy between my crisis and my creativity catalyzed a spontaneous spiritual awakening.[1] I made a quantum leap, from surviving to thriving. I was given to see that:

- Each of us has limitless creative potential;
- A thriving life is a *creation*, while surviving is a *reaction*;
- Love is the sculpting hand behind all positive, transformative creation;
- Creativity works at multiple levels: As one exercises it at the material level one can consciously access its immense power at the spiritual level;
- Creative initiatives are really the playgrounds or construction sites for the creation of oneself and one's life;
- Creativity is thereby a process of discovering and knowing oneself – one's higher self;
- Exercising creativity is, therefore, the soul-purpose (and the sole purpose) of a human life!

When I say 'creativity,' what do I mean? I mean something much larger and beyond the traditional sense typically referenced in everyday parlance. Yes, in material terms I do mean making tangible things of value to humanity,

---

[1] For some context on my spirituality, as well as how I use the terms spirit (or soul), Spirit, Universe, Love, etc., please refer to the Postface at the end of this book.

whether these are objects, or systems, or ways of seeing, doing and thinking about things, or ways of relating with others and touching lives...and so on.

In spiritual terms, though, creativity is our original blessing, our natural way of being, our healing, our return home. Like a seed germinating into the seedling and then into the plant and eventually into the tree it is meant to be, creativity is the action of allowing what is already in you, to emerge forth into the world. It is the process of tuning into, and then singing the music of your soul. It is the act of making quantum leaps to your higher self, allowing Love to chip and peel away the layers that obscure your inner light. As Michelangelo poignantly said, the sculptor's job is to chisel away the excess stone so that the sculpture already existing within the rock can be revealed.

And here's the magic – *You are at once both the sculptor and the sculpture*! As you create tangible, material works employing your singular spirit and imagination, these works in turn create you!

In a TED talk titled *Bring on the Learning Revolution*,[2] education expert Sir Ken Robinson makes a powerful statement that might easily go unnoticed. To me, it refers to this important idea of simultaneously being the creator and the created:

"We create our lives symbiotically as we explore our talents in relation to the circumstances they help to create for us."

---

[2] Watch: http://www.youtube.com/watch?v=r9LelXa3U_I

Creating yourself is not an act of self-improvement, the ubiquitous focus of most self-help books. Instead, it's about simply shedding and sculpting away the layers of conditioning and programming to reveal your already existing inner light – your soul's unique melody that you came here in body to express – allowing it to shine forth into the world. When you do this, your external reality is created in synchronicity, as a natural reflection of internal intention. As Dr. David Hawkins writes in *Power vs. Force*,

"There are no causes within the observable world...the observable world is a world of effects."

All causes are within human consciousness, and the effects are *creations* of conscious or unconscious intention. In a consciously creative life, physical health, resources, relationships, work, our impact on the world, are all naturally and organically created by our higher selves – moment-to-moment. And, as a result of each of us being and acting this way, universal consciousness is collectively created as a synergistic sum of our creative contributions!

In 2010, in a survey conducted by IBM of 1500 CEOs across sixty countries, the investigators drew the conclusion that "Creativity is the most essential skill for navigating an increasingly complex world."[3] While it is true that creativity is essential, the framing of creativity as a skill continues to perpetuate one of two myths – that it is either something augmentative that can be acquired, or that it is innately possessed by a lucky few. It is forgotten that creativity is the true, spiritual nature of human be-ing. In his inspiring book *The Element: How Finding Your Passion Changes Everything*, Sir Ken Robinson writes about the myths surrounding creativity. These are the beliefs that only some people are creative, that creativity is about special activities and domains, and that people are either creative or not.

So long as creativity is viewed as a skill, or as something relegated to the arts, or as the making of material objects or systems, instead of hailed as our very raison d'être, we will always fall short of expressing humanity's full potential. Creativity will flicker as the obscured flame within, instead of bringing Love and light into the world. We will miss doing what we're really here to do and be the way we're really here to be!

Creativity as spirituality – as an active practice of pure Love, as the expression of our true natures, as a return to home, as a union of spirit with Spirit – is rarely explored or discussed. In the third section of the moving book *The War of Art*, Steven Pressfield ventures into the territory of Spirit –

---

[3] *"Creativity Lessons from Charles Dickens and Steve Jobs,"* Anne Kreamer, HBR, March 27 2012.

Muses and angels, Mystery, the Void, the source of Infinite Wisdom, The Divine Ground – alluding to creativity as an exercise of the soul in dialogue with Spirit. And in the rare gem of a book, *Creativity: Where the Divine and the Human Meet,* radical theologian and Episcopal priest Matthew Fox writes:

"Creativity is not a noun or even a verb – it is a place, a space, a gathering, a union, a *where* – wherein the Divine powers of creativity and the human power of imagination meet."

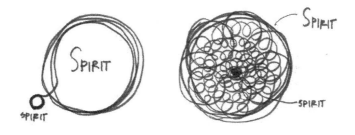

In my memoir of essays *Thrive! Falling in Love with Life*, I shared my intuitive insight that the meaning of "being created in the likeness of our Creator" is that we're in fractal self-similarity with our higher parent structure, and have, therefore, been seeded with the very same creative power, intended to be expressed through our be-ing. I was rather delighted to discover, well after the publication of my book (in which I had made a few daring, naive and imaginative forays into religious frameworks that I've neither been formally schooled or raised in, nor practice), that Fox concurs! He writes:

"When the Bible declares that we are made in the 'image and likeness' of the Creator, it is affirming that creativity is at our core just as it lies at the core of the Creator of all things. Not only the Bible but other traditions also celebrate our nearness to the creative powers of Divinity."

So, while this was hardly original insight on my part, it has been forgotten and must be re-cognized and re-membered for the expression of humanity's highest and truest potential.

If creation (however you believe the physics of it to have occurred) is seen as a Self-reflection by Spirit through manifesting Itself in physical form, then as fractal aspects of Spirit, every soul's creativity is a way of knowing and becoming its true self. Procreation, the most basic, corporeal, ubiquitous and prolific aspect of our creativity, beautifully clues us in to this understanding. Procreation helps us create in the most literal, physical dimension, in self-similarity with our bodily existence. In other dimensions of existence, then, creativity is the act of knowing and understanding ourselves in the corresponding dimensions. And as each of us gets to know ourselves through exercising our creativity, Spirit gets to know Itself through us!

Creativity, therefore, is the very purpose of human existence. As Fox puts it:

"'Creativity' may be the nearest one-word definition we possess for the essence of our humanity, for the true meaning of 'soul'... I propose that when all is said and done, *our true nature is our creativity*."

Creativity is the natural and unstoppable corollary to all that is intimately of Spirit – soul, self-reflection, inspiration, imagination, and most importantly, the expression of pure, unfettered Love. Creativity is not only our original blessing, but also our sacred *responsibility*, here in this life and on this planet. This means that when we don't exercise our innate creativity, we're not merely in benign neglect, but in outright rejection of our responsibility. In *The War of Art*, Steven Pressfield writes:

"...If you were meant to cure cancer or write a symphony or crack cold fusion and you don't do it, you not only hurt yourself, even destroy yourself...you hurt your children. You hurt me. You hurt the planet. You shame the angels who watch over you and you spite the Almighty, who created you and only you with your unique gifts, for the sole purpose of nudging the human race one millimeter farther along its path back to God...Creative work is not a selfish act or a bid for attention on the part of the actor. It's a gift to the world and every being in it. Don't cheat us of your contribution. Give us what you've got."

When we obscure our inner light and prevent Love from shining through, we allow fear to take over and create the illusion of suffering, not only for ourselves but for all others, because we exist in collective consciousness. We manifest all sorts of dis-ease, whether physical, psychological, social or environmental. Fox offers that we are all born in 'original blessing,' which is our creativity, and the only original sin is to deny our creativity, our intimate relationship with Spirit!

This book is my offering on creativity as fundamental human purpose – as self-reflection, as a manifest expression of Love, as an effort to know Truth, and as communion and co-creation with Spirit. Springing from this philosophical premise, the book offers concrete pointers and actions for the intentioned and disciplined practice of creativity, applicable to creating both oneself and physical works of meaning and value for the world. Whether you are looking to be creative in your work, relationships, parenting, community, or in building organizations and movements to transform the world, this book is for you. In each case, of course, what you will always really be creating, is the higher you! (And each time I address you, know that I also address myself.)

The first half of the book is all about building the foundation for a consciously creative life. In this section, the two chapters explore how our very first creation is our story about ourselves, and how this can be re-created from being driven by unconscious fear to being founded in conscious Love. In the second half of the book I explore how to source and balance the Yin and Yang aspects of creativity in complementarity and conjunction. For every necessary quality of the feminine creative principle within each of us, I explore a corresponding action of the masculine creative principle within, finding the integration and harmony between these two aspects that are required for the full expression of our immense creative power.

You are Michelangelo, and you are here to unveil David – the essential, true, higher you! All you need to do is to allow Love to be the sculpting agent and chisel away the excesses to reveal the light within, so that it may shine forth as your original gift to this world. What joy if this book does a small service in that awesome and inspiring endeavor!

PART I

BUILDING THE FOUNDATION

The fundamental difference between the accidental creative and the conscious creative is that the latter is constantly expanding her awareness, connecting with Spirit and intentionally accessing Love as the only creative force. Part I of the book explores how to build this strong foundation before actually exercising your creativity. Put in a single, simple sentence, it helps you quantum jump from fear to Love!

In the first chapter titled *Context: The Power of Your Story*, I explore how our very first creation is our story about ourselves, and I demonstrate how we can reframe this story, open it up to all possibility, and further, completely recreate it, all through conscious choice. I discuss how 'reactive storytelling' – storytelling as a reaction to the past – constructs a fear-based experience of the world as a place of lack, peril and injustice, fueling and perpetuating more of the very same, placing the past squarely in the future. And I explore how shifting into 'creative storytelling' – storytelling as a creation in and of the present – creates a Love-shaped world of soul, imagination, abundance and possibility.

In the second chapter titled *Preparation: Love as the Creative Force*, I explore ways in which Love can be accessed as the powerful, positive, sculpting agent shaping all conscious creation in one's life, replacing the unconscious, default creations of fear, especially at the level of underlying beliefs. As you'll discover, Love as understood here, is not the popular-culture notion, but the true power latent within each of us – that which *does* make the world go around!

1

CONTEXT

THE POWER OF YOUR STORY

"Don't be satisfied with stories, how things have gone with others. Unfold your own myth."

– Jalaluddin Rumi

"Creativity is a quantum leap in meaning, context, relationship and story."

– Deepak Chopra

"Creativity ... I call it exploring 'What If?' How would it look if we looked at the problem differently than we've been looking at it so far? That is creative imagination."

– Pir Vilayat Inayat Khan

1

CHANGE YOUR LIFE BY CHANGING YOUR STORY!

Everyone has a story. We're always telling stories, whether we're interacting with others or wrestling with the voices in our heads. I like to say that our story about ourselves is our very first, original, and most powerful act of creativity. We start creating in this way, unconsciously, as young as three years of age. And through our storytelling, we are powerfully putting into motion all sorts of creation!

Your story is powerful because it presents who you are today and provides the basis for agency in the world. It has the potential to touch, move and inspire others. The rarely leveraged creative opportunity in storytelling, however, is the choice to consciously transform the old story once its value and power are exhausted. Marianne Williamson writes in *The Law of Divine Compensation,*

"Spiritual growth involves giving up the stories of your past so the universe can write a new one."

I've discovered that since the material world is a playground for our souls' creations, material reality is, in truth, a reflection and creation of our individual and collective storytelling, rather than the other way around! This one little secret, this flip of cause and effect, can transform your life forever, as it has mine. This is what Dr. David Hawkins, whom I quoted in the Introduction, means when he says that the observable world only has effects, no causes. Because we don't typically recognize our creative power, most of us shape our stories as a reaction or response to material reality, narrating accounts of it, not realizing that our stories can *create* material reality. Our creative power allows us to transcend the past story so that a new one can be written in the present – at every turn – to create new futures as a natural outcome of the more present, more consciously chosen story. As Robert Kennedy once said,

> "There are those who look at things the way they are, and ask why...I dream of things that never were, and ask why not?"

To be able to fully harness our immense creative power for consciously and lovingly shaping our realities, let's explore storytelling in some depth. Let's first explore how our storytelling reflects our existing programming – perceptions, assumptions, expectations, beliefs and feelings – and how these essentially create our present circumstances, and further, limit what we can and cannot create. Then, let's explore how to step into possibility, how to intentionally and periodically create a blank slate so that possibilities for new stories become unlimited. Finally, let's see how we can consciously choose a new story from among all possibilities, based on soulful vision and purpose rather than reaction to circumstance and perceived limitation.

Open your heart to creating a new story!

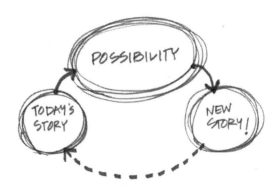

2

JUMP TO CREATIVE STORYTELLING FROM REACTIVE STORYTELLING

One of the quantum leaps I've made is to stumble upon the idea of creative storytelling, instead of the habitual, reactive storytelling in which we typically engage. By the way, these are terms I've happily made up, but I know you'll get my drift as you read on!

What do I mean by creative storytelling? Well, anything creative is *generative* – it is coded with possibility, imbued with the energy of limitless potential. Like a seed coded with the secrets of becoming a tree, or DNA coded with mysterious scripts for incredible human talent, anything creative has the power to generate – everything from nothing. When we tell stories, which is pretty much every time we open our mouths to talk, we can choose the opportunity to create – that is, to hold possibility – or we can continue to merely react to current circumstance and material reality. I'm forever in awe of this powerful opportunity for daily creativity!

What if your storytelling were *always* creative? What if your story were to authentically and genuinely describe your present moment in terms of the creative potential it holds – the seed to generate something with Love, soul, imagination, and vision? What if it were to paint a picture of possibility, compelling yourself and another to together stare up at the blue sky or the full moon, and simply dream? What if your story could always invite the listener's soul into a *real* conversation, a collaboration, a co-creation with your soul?

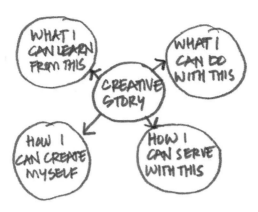

When spirit meets spirit in this way, it is then that we can say that *inspiration* has been experienced! We are inspired because Spirit Itself has entered into this co-creation between souls, holding hands with us, penetrating us with high frequency energy in a shared melody, blessing and guiding us into positive creation. We finally enter our soul purpose, our sacred contract, to be creative, individually and together.

Presently, almost all of human storytelling is reactive. It is based in reactivity to the past or in analysis of what's 'wrong' or lacking. In the profound and transformative book *The Art of Possibility*, Boston Philharmonic conductor, Benjamin Zander and psychotherapist, Rosamund Stone Zander explore phenomena of human perception to demonstrate how our programming leads us to see a map of the world, not really the world itself, and how the map we choose to create conforms to our efforts toward survival. In other words, our story maps aren't designed to help us thrive; rather they are *reactive* strategies and tactics to survive, meeting what we perceive as our needs against threats. Another way of saying it is that our story maps are typically fear-based, not based in Love – soul, imagination, abundance, vision and possibility.

Take the simple example of most activist or political agendas. The first thing in the storytelling is to describe the lack – what is missing, what is in serious deficit, what is dreadfully wrong – and then the proposed policy or solution or movement that is supposed to improve this lack, to fill this void, to better this terrible deficit, is duly offered. I frequently ponder that most of my advanced academic experience consisted of reactive storytelling as well! For instance, whether one is writing a research paper or grant proposal, one is encouraged to first conduct a literature review, run an analysis, find the research 'gap,' and then found one's big idea in this specialized, limited, narrow crevice of *lack*. Wow!

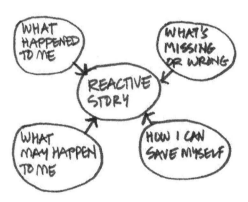

Reactive storytelling is omnipresent in our everyday language as well, in apparently harmless ways, but it is actually insidious and limiting to potential and possibility, because it causes what the Zanders call a "downward spiral." Reflect a moment on how we record history, how we conduct our journalism, and how we talk about our family, relationships, or careers. Talk to someone new at a social gathering, and she will immediately ask you, "Where are you from?" or "What do you do?", as if these markers of your past or present are any true introduction to the creative, limitless soul that you are. And my guess is, instead of leaping at the opportunity to be creative in your response, nine times out of ten you find yourself falling into the trap of reactive storytelling – telling stories about yourself as a reflection of your past, of your history, of what has "happened to you" and brought you to this present moment. Only rarely will your storytelling give the listener a chance to truly connect with your naked soul, let alone glimpse it. No, instead, *your* mask will politely converse with *her* mask, and you'll both go home having exchanged stories that don't really matter, that have limited generative potential, that didn't enlighten or inspire anybody in any way.

Here's the irony. No matter what good cause an activist or political or academic agenda seeks to 'fight for' or 'solve,' it will often largely perpetuate more of the same, or a variant or derivative of it. There may be wonderful improvements from this kind of approach; there will be change and evolution, but there won't be *transformation*. This is because the energetic quality of this kind of storytelling is founded in limitation, lack and prevention – essentially in fear. And because energy of a certain frequency simply takes different forms within the same bandwidth if you will, all outcomes will carry the same essential quality of fear and lack even when they appear to be reasonably good improvements. I sense that this is what Einstein attempted to convey when he famously said,

"No problem can be solved from the same level of consciousness that created it."

This is also the very thesis of Deepak Chopra's latest book, *Spiritual Solutions*. In it he writes:

"The secret is that the level of the problem is never the level of the solution."

So, to quantum jump into a thriving, creative life, all we need to do is make a leap in consciousness! But, how do we make this leap? Here, a metaphor that serves me well comes from the biology of the caterpillar-to-butterfly transformation. During this process, after the worm cocoons, it disintegrates into a gooey, oozy mass of cells. Then suddenly, one or two cells appear, seemingly out of thin air, with a completely different character from the original worm cells. In fact, the ooze of old cells even attempts to attack these new cells in an auto-immune response. These new cells are called 'imaginal' cells – because they appear as if from pure imagination, from just about nowhere! Although some are successfully destroyed, one by one, the imaginal cells that do make it, connect with each other to form clusters, and eventually, the clusters connect with each other as well. The critical mass of imaginal cells grows, and the new paradigm is now established. The butterfly is born!

In other words, the trans-formation of a caterpillar into a butterfly is exactly that – the *transcendence* of old patterning to make a quantum leap into an entirely new and different creature. This reveals that metamorphosis is not a derivative or incremental process but an imaginative one, and this insight holds the key for us to understand the difference between evolution and transformation. Evolution is incremental improvement, but transformation is ongoing creation!

If you can go along with the analogy of the imaginal cell, it all begins with a rather simple choice – the choice to drop the storyline of the past like a hot potato, and make the leap into possibility, using nothing but your imagination! Whoosh!

23

In *Spiritual Solutions*, Deepak Chopra writes:

"Although it may seem that it takes long experience on the spiritual path to reach pure awareness, the truth is exactly the opposite. At every moment, pure awareness is in contact with you, sending creative impulses. All that matters is how open you are to the answers being presented."

When you become open to higher awareness and possibility, the imaginal cells of your new being will begin emerging as if out of nowhere. At first your old patterning may attack them in an auto-immune response, but soon the new cells of imagination will strengthen in numbers and critical mass. The dots will connect, and suddenly you'll be a butterfly!

I invite you to one of my favorite activities, which is to imagine for a moment the Wright Brothers dreaming up the airplane. (I see it as my advantage that I haven't researched or read much about their process, so that I can allow my imagination and intuition to conduct this inquiry, and I humbly accept any allegations of hopeless naiveté.) Do you think the Wright Brothers sat around storytelling about the terrible gap in human capability – that humans can't fly? I'm betting not. Rather, they were likely inspired by the birds in the sky, soaring in the fluffy clouds, that much closer to the radiant sun...and they *created* a story in their imaginations, of a soaring human soul. With this idea conceived in spirit, *just because*, not motivated by solving for a lack or void or hole, they went on to use their analytical skills in service to the Muse. They created a vision first, and then executed it. That their creative invention *did* better many human lives (as well as damage others in wars and the like) is likely a *byproduct* of their service of the creative calling, the Muse. I would venture that they weren't seeking explicitly to improve the sorry state of humanity, but were fulfilling the spiritual drive to be inspired by something in Nature, envision possibility, and then connect the dots in new ways to turn that possibility into material reality. In other words, they were simply being creative, for the sake of creativity alone.

Now, you may be thinking that this is all nice and dandy for pie-in-the-sky inventions, but what about *real* problems such as poverty, hunger, illiteracy, feudality, violence and oppression, depletion of natural systems, and so on? Again, I remind us that reality is a reflection of our imaginations. We only have the current reality that we have, because we haven't been adequately imaginative, creative and loving as human beings; we have been reactive in fear of survival, pillaging and hoarding material, intellectual and spiritual resources, and creating gross imbalances in the world. So, I offer that in all these challenging arenas too, true transformation occurs at the level of soulful, loving, courageous imagination, not at the level of deficit-based thinking, righting wrongs, and willful problem solving.

Starting with our daily lives, in everyday terms it is pretty easy to practice creative storytelling. In fact, it is also great fun! In *The Art of Possibility*, the very foundation of creating possibility is the practice, "It's All Invented." Zander and Zander offer,

"It's all invented anyway, so we might as well invent a story or framework of meaning that enhances our quality of life and the life of those around us."

All this requires is to constantly tap into the powers of our imaginations to step into possibility, and bring a gentle awareness around our habitual tendency for reactive storytelling. For instance, in the Creativity Workshops I coach, we practice getting to know each other at an imaginary social gathering, responding creatively to questions such as, "Where are you from?" or "What do you do?" By inviting imagination, curiosity and humor, participants are able to come up with responses and ways of conversing that are far more engaging, inviting, authentic, inspiring and generative than anything we would typically hear at such gatherings.

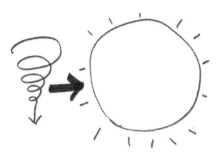

One workshop participant's creative response to the question, "Where are you from?" was, "I am new to Seattle and I'm still finding my way. What inspires you in the city that I can explore more?" Such a response immediately creates opportunity and possibility. It is generative, so it is creative. We also practice inquiring about others in ways that create possibility for *them*. Some examples are, "So, what rocks your boat?" "Who do you know in this party that inspires you?" and so on. And we practice doing two-minute 'TED talks' about ourselves, describing our life purpose and current creative projects. In each such exercise, participants are able to find language and expression for their storytelling that create possibility and sow the generative seed that can sprout into transformative outcomes.

REFLECTIONS

1 What is your typical response when someone asks you, "Where are you from?" Can you think of different ways to answer this question, ways that create possibility for you as well as for your listener?

2 What is your response to "What do you do?" How could you answer this question differently? Can there be ways to answer it that create possibility for you?

3 Take a look at your different responses to both questions. Choose the ones that open your world to opportunity and possibility. The next time you are asked these questions, practice answering with your chosen response(s) and observe what happens in the conversation.

3
ASK YOURSELF: WHAT IS TRUTH?

Do keep in mind that not for a moment am I suggesting that creative storytelling is about prevaricating, or about obscuring or evading the truth. To the contrary, creative storytelling is about *uncovering* Truth – the truth of our purer natures, of our creative potential, of our essential core of

Love. It is about wiping the fog off the mirror to see one's true reflection, one's spirit, beyond the layers of conditioning, programming and material-reality baggage. It is about chipping away the debris of excess stone – of falsehood and illusion that we carry around as our fear-based perceptions, assumptions, expectations and beliefs – so that the true sculpture latent within, can be revealed. In fact, creative storytelling challenges our attachment to a past story, and the mistaken assumption that our story of the past is 'the truth'!

So, what is Truth? This appears to be such a huge question, the question of all time that philosophers, artists, scientists and mystics have sought to answer. Had there been one right answer, we would've had a one-liner (or a unified theory in physics) by now! That alone should tell you that *creating* Truth is why we're here, and that creativity is our purpose in service of this endeavor. And I have a strong inkling that Truth is closely related to Love. Do you?

Stepping aside for a moment from the grandeur of this question lest we become overwhelmed and lost, let's consider how we use the term 'the truth' in everyday parlance. For one, we confuse storytelling with Truth. "Tell me the truth about what really happened!" a parent might scold her child; or, "I'm not convinced he was telling me the truth," someone might say. Here's the thing – the moment we ask someone for 'the truth,' what we're always getting is their story. What we should really ask is, "Tell me your version of the story!"

Next, in our underlying, unquestioned belief-system, we equate Truth with physicality, with material reality. We've collectively signed up for the belief that what is physical must be true, and conversely, if it isn't physical, then it's not true – it's even 'immaterial'! So, when a young child uses her imagination and explores fantasyland, claiming to have fallen down the rabbit hole, we're afraid the child needs correction since none of what she makes up is physically real or true.

"Don't make up lies!" we might chide her, even if gently, and we inadvertently train her to shut down her imagination, conditioning her with our own belief system of equating physicality or material reality with Truth. We stunt the incredible, limitless potential of her imagination to *create* new reality! And yet we all know that the power that keeps us all in motion – Love – *is* real, because we experience it, even if there is no physical proof of its existence. (As an aside, it occurs to me as I write this, that all human suffering essentially stems from incessantly seeking proof of Love!)

Third, we forget that our telling of 'the truth' is necessarily contextual and relational. If I'm honestly telling you exactly how I experienced something, of course I am telling you *my* truth! But is my truth the same as yours? Would you have experienced the same situation or incident or circumstance or person exactly the same way? Does there exist any reality beyond our subjective experience of things? And further, does reality exist outside the space of relationship between you and I, you the listener and I the teller, and vice-versa?

In philosopher Martin Buber's important essay *Ich und Du* (translated into English as *I and Thou*), the premise of all human existence is encounter, interaction, or relationship. Another exploration of Truth within the space of human interaction is found in the historic dialogue between two extraordinary Nobel Laureates, Albert Einstein and Rabindranath Tagore. When Einstein suggested the possibility of an absolute truth independent of human consciousness, Tagore responded:

"...this world is a human world – the scientific view of it is also that of the scientific man...Truth, which is one with the Universal Being, must necessarily be human, otherwise whatever we individuals realize as true can never be called truth...What we call truth lies in the rational harmony between the subjective and objective aspects of reality, both of which belong to the super-personal man."[4]

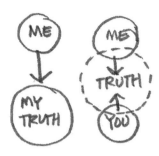

So, as far as I'm concerned, whether or not there is a single objective Truth (– both science and most religions aspire to one –), is a moot point because so long as we, as humans, exist *in relationship* with each other and with the Universe, then all that matters is that we are always relating our unique truths to one another; we are telling genuine stories about our (inter- and intra-) personal experiences. Truth comes into being moment-to-moment through our experience of the world, in relation to it and to each other within it. And our interactions occur in several dimensions beyond material reality, which we don't yet fully consciously understand.

Therefore, for the purposes of our discussion here, I propose that 'the truth' is always a story, revealed in a relational interaction with the Universe. Further, I propose that I come closest to Truth when I experience and relate with life with an open, courageous, loving heart, and share my

---

[4] The full dialogue that occurred on July 14, 1930 can be read in the book, *Science and the Indian Tradition: When Einstein Met Tagore*. An excerpt can be found at: http://www.brainpickings.org/index.php/2012/04/27/when-einstein-met-tagore/

experience with you, with as much authenticity, vulnerability and Love as I can! *That* is when I am telling you a creative, generative story. That is Truth, and it is created in that moment of genuine, relational experience.

This exploration of 'the truth' is significant to exercising creativity because as soon as we attempt to step out of reactive storytelling into creative storytelling, our voice of reason (that can be fear in a rather clever disguise!) is likely to challenge us. "You're obscuring the truth!" it'll accuse. I witness this all the time with both myself and those I coach. This adherence to 'the truth' is really an attachment to one story versus other possible stories. We're attached to a certain version of the story and firmly label it 'the truth,' because somehow that particular version serves our conditioned selves in some latent or overt way. It could be that the particular story aligns with our underlying beliefs, to which we're vehemently attached. Or that it fulfills our expectations. Or it confirms our latent perceptions and assumptions. Very often, the unconsciously chosen story helps us be right about something, or provides us the comfort and security of status quo. It helps us feel good in some way.

A situation that merits special mention in this context is one in which we have suffered egregious injustices. What if we were robbed? Or bombed? Or beaten and raped? Our attachment to the story of victimhood becomes strong because our very survival was threatened, and the idea that creating a thriving life might require relinquishing the old story becomes equal to further wronging oneself! On top of this, our attachment to the concept of justice makes it even harder to transform our story.

I have personally been there, so I speak to you from the depths of my heart. I'll explore our attachment to rightness and justice in the following chapter, but for now, consider stretching yourself with me to the possibility that even with such difficult and painful histories, creating a new story doesn't mean denying your past, but *transcending* it. It doesn't mean looking away from past reality and its problems, but looking *beyond* them. It means knowing that even though your mortal self may have suffered serious damage, your higher, spiritual self remains eternally unharmed, untouched, pure and fertile, able to create everything from nothing. If you can consider occupying this limitless possibility of you, you'll see how being in this knowing is actually far more liberating, (re)generative, empowering and powerful than being morally right about your wrongdoers or the wrong done unto you. I often offer to those I coach and witness, including myself, "What happened was morally wrong but spiritually correct."

Returning to all the reasons for taking comfort in an existing story, whatever the payoff may be, when we cannot separate our story from Truth, we're merely stuck in our attachment to one particular story, and are refusing to explore other possibilities. The thing is, our perceptions, expectations, assumptions, beliefs and feelings can all be re-created, and they *must be* – all the time – as we transform. So, as soon as we connect with what we're really attached to that's keeping us stuck in one single story, we become free to create a new story!

One of the ways I love to practice the separation of story from Truth is to create what I like to call a story map – a map of all possible stories, different narratives of the same event or situation – all truthful. Participants in the Creativity Workshops create this story map with great enthusiasm and gusto, when they see the difference between reactive and creative storytelling, and experience how much possibility opens up for them in the latter.

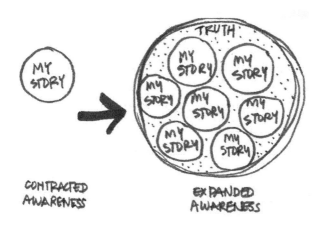

For example, one participant was exploring how to best express what she does, in order to kick-start her creative and entrepreneurial venture. Trained in Reiki and passionate about healing with energy work, she also delights in making jewelry, and is deeply attracted to the energetic and healing properties of various gemstones. As you might expect, she is also connected to the power of Love within her, and sees service as an important attitude in her presence on this planet. When she explored her story map and connected the dots in different ways between her various interests, passions and skills, here are some of the storylines she came up with. "I am a jewelry designer and Reiki practitioner." "I am a designer and healer." "I serve through healing and design." "I design healing."...And so on. Once she had mapped these various options, she became free to choose the most generative one as her story.

In a personal example, I've used the story map to explore what once used to be a significant health issue. Various versions on the story map might be as follows. "I've always had bad headaches that simply won't go away." "I have a chronic condition of migraines." "I experience migraine pain often." "I am improving a lot, as I only have migraine pain every few weeks now." "My frequent pain helps me prioritize the important things in my life." "I am learning to live fully and joyfully in spite of pain." "I am healing and becoming free of pain."... And so on. Through the years, the story has evolved, and with it, so has my reality, because I have created it moment-to-moment. (Of course I have made other changes too, in diet and lifestyle, but those have organically revealed themselves in response to the story I chose!)

Imagine what all can open up through the mapping of all possible stories that our imagination can afford at any given moment! First, we become free of the attachment to the concept of 'the truth,' that keeps us stuck in one place. We also get underneath the attachment to connect with the perceptions, assumptions, expectations, beliefs and feelings that defined our old story. And then we begin to question and explore these underlying motivations, for possible transformation. We become open to greater possibility.

From the story map of possible stories, we can spot the stories that are founded in Love (instead of fear), and contain the highest generative potential. Now we've shifted from reactivity to creativity. And finally, we can intentionally *choose* the most empowering, loving, generative story! By opening up choice, what previously seemed like a given, fixed situation becomes open to transformation, to re-creation. The new, consciously chosen, present story is always creative – because it *creates* the future in the present!

Discerning Truth apart from our storytelling about something or its material reality – a situation, circumstance, event, or person – is a creative practice for a lifetime. It requires constant awareness, courage, and the opening of one's heart to absolutely all possibility.

REFLECTIONS

1   Think of a situation in which you believe you were wronged by someone. Write down your story about what happened.

2   Now, think about the other person's potential story. Write it down.

3   Are there any other possible stories for you and for her? Shift vantage points, stretch your imagination, even try to laugh and have fun if possible. Choose new types of words that show you are the creator of the story rather than merely the actor or victim in it. Write down all possible stories.

4   You now have your story map! Which story do you think is 'the truth'? Are the others untrue? Do you see a story that can help you become unstuck and let go? Do you see a story that creates the greatest possibility? Observe how the new story is different from the original story you started with.

4

BECOME AWARE OF THE UNCONSCIOUS CREATIVITY OF FEAR

Reactive storytelling – based on 'the truth' founded in a story of the past – is a creation of fear.

In the absence of a cultivated awareness of and a connection with our innate nature of Love and creativity, fear is the default creative force, creating away on behalf of our souls! I've written quite a bit about fear in my previous book *Thrive!*, and building on those insights, I present my most current ones here, along with concrete, actionable pointers.

First, what is fear? At the moment of this writing, I offer that at the most fundamental level, fear is the feeling of absence – the illusion that we are separate and alone – the genesis of ego.[5] It is the forgetting of Oneness and Presence. We can all imagine or relate to the desperate feeling of separation and absence in a little child if she were to suddenly believe that she has no parent. When we think we're alone, with absolutely no benevolence watching out for our highest and best, we panic about our survival. And much of our doing, even when apparently 'positive,' can become motivated and guided by this powerful underlying force – the fear of survival. And this is so regardless of our stated beliefs about divinity or

---

[5] In common parlance, the word ego is often used interchangeably with hubris or arrogance. I do not mean it in this way, even though the ego does manifest in such attributes. I use the word ego to mean all forms of identity that separate us from 'the other' – a separation that does serve a functional purpose in the material world, but can cause all sorts of suffering if not understood as a temporary illusion. Spiritually speaking, the ego is the foundation of separation consciousness – from each other, from Spirit, from Oneness, and only its transcendence returns us home to Love and Spirit.

Spirit; whether or not we believe in a higher power, in actual practice, most of us are unconsciously programmed to operate in knee-jerk reactivity and self-protection from the latent assumption that we are separate, alone and abandoned.

Fear is the supreme creator of all suffering, and the concomitant surviving mindset, which operates under the assumption that the world is a place of lack, peril, loss and injustice. To the survival mindset, all of these things must be 'fought against' or 'eradicated' for human survival and happiness. (This may be the case even with apparent 'positive thinkers,' because this fear-based process of creation is unconscious.) A survival-based belief system creates a negative energy field, matching which all our circumstances and material reality also get created. Fear designs reality as an elaborate, chronic, unrelenting obstacle course, to which we must be hyper-alert and react constantly in order to stay alive and safe, and accomplish this all alone too! It creates the fight-or-flight response, putting our sympathetic nervous systems in overdrive and causing suffering through disease, negativity, angst, cynicism, ennui, apathy, withdrawal, depression, violence and hatred...and worst of all, more fear. We become chronically re-active, instead of creative.

The power of fear is exponentially multiplied by our habitually reactive storytelling. Because such storytelling is founded in lack – in absence – it is, by definition, both a form and a perpetrator of fear! As I've alluded to before, this includes most activist and political manifestos of today, no matter what good cause they are seeking to 'fight for.' And the same kind of storytelling is omnipresent in our recording of history, in our media reporting, in our academic training, and just about everywhere in our everyday narratives on family, relationships, or career. Thus, fear continues to create more of the same, placing our pasts squarely in our futures, leaving us wondering why we are stuck in the same patterns, individually and collectively.

But, because as aspects of Spirit, we are in truth, *not* alone or abandoned, and because only Oneness is true, it follows that all fear is illusion, and only Love is true. Marianne Williamson writes in *The Law of Divine Compensation*:

"Thoughts placed in the service of fear deactivate the Law of Divine Compensation. Why? Because they are *unloving*. They are attack thoughts, and miracles only flow through the auspices of loving thought. It is love and love alone that gives us the power to transcend the lower thought forms and appearances of the mortal world. Only love of our self and others gives us the divine authority to reset the trajectories by which our life unfolds."

The key to shifting into our conscious, creative power of Love is to cultivate a gentle, compassionate awareness of our fear in action.

The first thing to notice about fear is that it operates through our ego – our sense of separateness and individuality. So long as we exist in physical body, our ego exists as well, and it is necessary too! The ego is what allows us to relate to one another and the world, because only from the perspective of our separateness can we experience relationship with 'the other.' This is the very essence of the experience of the material world. So, the ego serves a very important role – it is *through* this illusory and temporary experience of discrete separateness that we can remember, realize and return to our greater Oneness! It is through the experience of darkness that we recognize Light. So also, it is through transcending the false sense of aloneness that we reconnect with Spirit.

So, the ego is essentially indestructible in our material existence, and that's a fine thing, for it makes our lives the rich experiences that they are. The only thing to compassionately observe is that the ego is the vehicle through which fear operates, for it continuously reinforces the illusion of separateness and aloneness. This is, after all, its very job! And this fear-ego entity has many, many clever disguises and avatars. If you're pretty self-aware, you may easily recognize 'negative' avatars like shame, pride, anger, self-critique and blame, jealousy, envy, doubt, anxiety, gloom, withdrawal, addiction, self-justification, defensiveness, resistance, procrastination, and so on.

But here's the catch. The fear-ego complex also takes the form of apparently good things; it has several 'positive' avatars too. I have no doubt that this is going to be confronting for you, so hold on tight! Topping this list is ego masquerading as the voice of reason – the analytical, rational mind that makes the 'right decisions' for us. It perpetrates itself in 'reasonable' beliefs and values-based constructs about goodness, justice, and right and wrong. It appears in constructs of the self, such as "that's just me" or "that's just not me," or other labels of identity, whether cultural, social, professional, ideological, political, or religious. It disguises itself rather cleverly as perfectionism and inauthentic affectations of humility or responsibility.

The ego also sneaks up as the 'tug of the heart' in the misconstrued conception of love as need or as a function of another, rather than the intrinsic nature of the soul. And the ego perpetuates as the body and its needs, including illness, allergies and chronic conditions (yes, my migraines included). It lurks in little, apparently harmless habits, such as obsessively checking email and Facebook, as that tiny spoonful of sugar, a few minutes of sensationalism on TV, and so on. And amazingly, the ego even projects itself as other people in our lives – as our anxious parents 'worried for our benefit,' as our kids and even pets who embody our fears and turn into obstacles in our creative paths, or as our friends who like us 'just the way we are,' acting as if they stand to lose were we to truly transform. (All these projections are our egos' creations, and therefore solely our responsibility, not that of others.)

Like the black-suit-clad men in the film *The Matrix*, ego's various avatars multiply at the rate of bunnies. They are indestructible; just when you think you've decimated one, there's another one popping up in the landscape! Most humorously of all, whose voice do you think tells you to overcome your ego? (Or for that matter, whose voice is writing this book, and whose voice is reacting in your head as you read it?) That too is of the ego! So, the endeavor here is not to fight the ego, for we will only succeed in energizing and strengthening it, and its fear-based reactions. The effort is to fully embrace the experience of ego while remaining vigilantly, yet gently and light-heartedly observant of the fear it perpetrates, as well as the related fallacies that arise from this fear.

Because fear is the feeling of absence and the forgetting of Presence, Presence alone can help. The moment we become present, the feeling of absence has no choice but to disappear! The moment we shine Light, darkness must become illuminated. The moment we become observant, we become the creator, not merely the actor. And consequently, our energy field naturally rises in frequency, automatically increasing our access to pure creativity. By remembering and becoming present to all the assistance, benevolence and goodness in the world, we can always remain in Love. Instead of fighting fear and ego, all we need to do is to bring a gentle awareness and humor to their nature, their machinations and their cleverly disguised avatars.

To help expand awareness and bring Presence to fear, I find that it is most productive to inquire: What does fear *feel* like? This is because, once we're aware of the subtle feelings generated by fear, we can allow ourselves to fully and wholeheartedly feel the feelings and thereby *transmute* them into creative foil. I've discovered that when I feel the feelings instead of running from them or intellectualizing them away, what's revealed behind the temporary reactions is always a blank canvas – nothingness – which invokes a deep sense of peace and all possibility. This practiced transmutation of our fearful feelings and the (re)generation of the blank canvas, allow Love, our true creative power, to gently take hold. And as soon as Love takes its place in the driver's seat of our lives, we can return home to our creativity. The imaginal cells are born, and soon become established as the new paradigm!

In practicing Presence, I find that my body is my best friend in first alerting me that I am in fear, and then in helping me transmute the fear. Fear feels like the knot in the stomach, the dry throat, the sweaty palms, the short breath, the quickening heart, or the pulsing temples. (Yes, excitement is an avatar of fear! Only *enthusiasm* is Love.) More extremely, fear might feel like the heavy sadness in my heart, ready to gush out as tears, or the chronic fatigue that might keep me lingering in bed. Connecting with these feelings not only alerts me to the fear, but also allows me to fully feel it, by embracing my body as a channel for its transmutation. Like a town might respond to a growing snowstorm or raincloud, I can allow fear to pass through the 'town' of my body, my soul standing by as the still, observant, gentle, neutral, good-humored and loving witness. For me, practices such as yoga, walking, meditation, singing classical music and painting are excellent avenues for this physical clearing and transmutation to occur without becoming mired in the analytics of the busy mind.

Quite paradoxically, this acceptance of fear allows it to flow through the body without becoming converted into either constructs and beliefs of the mind, or into disease and blocks in the body, both of which occur when we don't feel the feelings, enabling fear to strengthen and perpetuate at a visceral level. As soon as fear has flowed through me as the passing storm, its illusion passes too, and I can return to the blank canvas on which Love's soulful and imaginative creations of possibility can be painted!

By bringing Presence to fear's creative power, its operative mechanics and various clever avatars, and most importantly, by practicing the transmutation of fear through the feelings in our bodies, we become liberated to return home – to Love, to possibility, to creativity, to Spirit. Our faith in all that is good, benevolent, and generative is firmly reinstated. And we can consciously choose to channel Love, our pure nature, as the power behind our creativity, fulfilling our sacred contract with Spirit.

2

PREPARATION

LOVE AS THE CREATIVE FORCE

"Love is the only reality and it is not a mere sentiment. It is the ultimate truth that lies at the heart of creation."

– Rabindranath Tagore

"The Atonement means putting love first. In everything. In business as well as everything else. You're in business to spread love. Your screenplay should spread love. Your hair salon should spread love. Your agency should spread love. Your life should spread love. The key to a successful career is realizing that it's not separate from the rest of your life, but is rather an extension of your most basic self. And your most basic self is love."

– Marianne Williamson

"The best pieces of creativity…don't start off as 'product.' They don't start life out as things. They start out as acts of Love."

– Hugh Macleod

.

1
RECOGNIZE YOUR TRUE NATURE AS LOVE

As souls, Love is our essential nature. Because you are an aspect of Spirit, you are made of Love, and of nothing else. All fear, the absence of Love, is a mere illusion, a temporary affliction in material reality. And here's something I'll offer with enthusiasm: The degree of expression of our full creative potential is related *only* to the extent of our ability to recognize and embody our true nature of Love![6] The illusion of ego and fear temporarily obscures our true natures, limiting our creative potential. Reacting and unconsciously creating our individual and collective reality with fear is the original and *only* sin, if there were even one!

So, to act in the original blessing of Spirit, we must awaken to our true nature as Love, and Love alone. Such awakening *is* enlightenment. In *The Law of Divine Compensation* Marianne Williamson writes,

"To self-identify according to your spiritual rather than material reality is enlightenment. From this perspective you see that you are the light."

To recognize, accept and embody our nature as Love is to live in our limitless spiritual and creative power, rather than become lost and mired in the illusory world of ego-separation, material reality and circumstance. When we embody our true

---

[6] If you're finding yourself wondering if or how this applies to your enterprise, whether a business, organization or educational institution, read *Love is the Killer App* by Tim Sanders or *Wired to Care* by Dev Patnaik. Or subscribe to Hugh Macleod's blog gapingvoid at www.gapingvoid.com

nature of Love in our way of being and doing in the world, we become a willing partner to Spirit. We naturally step into our full creative potential to co-create material reality with Spirit!

Why is it at all challenging to awaken to and embody Love, when it is our true nature as souls to begin with? Especially when 'love' is such a ubiquitous word, the stuff of romantic films, novels and poetry? Well, what we've termed 'love' in the reactionary, fear-driven consciousness is simply another clever avatar of ego and fear. Such 'love' is founded in need, expectation, obligation, ownership, manipulation, and control. It isn't true Love, which is about complete liberation, about letting go and letting be. This doesn't mean that true Love doesn't engender relationships of form, such as committed partnerships of various kinds, whether intimate or organizational. This only means that relationships based in true Love are between complete and sovereign beings who, at the level of spirit, depend on each other for *nothing*, even if material, mental, emotional and spiritual resources are productively, honorably and synergistically shared. There is co-creation, yet no co-dependency. True Love knows without a doubt, Wholeness, Abundance, and Gratitude.[7] It knows to be in Resonance with the supreme creativity of Spirit, employing the power of relationship to co-create together in the service of greater good.

Besides being conditioned in false constructs of 'love,' embodying true Love is also challenging because one must (not reject but) transcend reason, which is a discontinuous, quantum leap to make within human consciousness. In a state of reason, one's compassion is still a mental, righteous compassion, and one loves the world through activism and making things happen externally. In very high-integrity reason, one may even be able to move toward acceptance and non-

---

[7] See more on these principles in the last essay of this chapter, *Sing your highest and best melody!*

judgmental forgiveness. An example is Mahatma Gandhi's untiring call for nonviolence as the only way to achieve freedom for India. He held firm in spite of being thrown off a train for his skin color, in spite of events such as the massacre of Jallianwala Bagh and other inhuman cruelties of the British Raj. Gandhi's approach was, for the most part, *unreasonable*, calling for unconditional acceptance of the life of all beings, including one's oppressors.

Love, however, transcends even acceptance. In Love there is no deficit, fault or wrong to begin with, even as moral frameworks are recognized, valued and duly upheld. So, you can see why making the leap from reason to Love is exceedingly challenging. Very few of us can hold that highly intuitive, unquestioningly faithful, unreasonable frequency state.

In *Power vs. Force*,[8] psychiatrist, physician and mystic Dr. David Hawkins exemplifies the difference between power (based in Love) and force (based in fear) in various human endeavors at the organizational scale. Taking the example of politics, he writes:

"...consider the difference between politicians and statesmen. Politicians, operating out of expediency, rule by

---

[8] Dr. Hawkins had the largest psychiatric practice in the United States for 50 years, at one time, treating almost 1000 patients a year. In 1973, he reported the work he was doing in the book *Orthomolecular Psychiatry* co-authored with two-time Nobel Laureate Linus Pauling. Later, using applied kinesiology (a method that does not stand to scientific scrutiny), he developed the 'scale of consciousness' – a logarithmic scale to calibrate different states of being in human consciousness. Labeling and categorizing human consciousness by using 'scientific rigor' seems a bit like using reason to transcend reason, but I've gained some important qualitative insights from Dr. Hawkins's work. These are: (a) There is Universal intelligence in the collective consciousness that can be tapped, and (b) There are points of transcendence in human consciousness, such as Reason to Love, which can significantly transform human experience in material reality.

force...Statesmen represent true power, ruling by inspiration, teaching by example, and standing by self-evident principle. Statesmen invoke the nobility that resides within all men and unifies them through what can be best termed 'the heart.' Although the intellect is easily fooled, the heart recognizes the truth. Where the intellect is limited, the heart is unlimited; where the intellect is intrigued by the temporary, the heart is only concerned with the permanent."

I find that Love is a state of very high energy frequency, not impossible for many of us to reach, but challenging to hold and sustain as our steady state. It's like constantly singing our highest and best melody! Although it is challenging, the delightful thing is that even mere glimpses of our true nature as souls of Love, are sufficient to spark and unlock our creativity. By founding all thought, choice and action in our heart-center, by channeling Love as the creative agent, we are able to create value through our innate gifts, learned skills and other resources. Ultimately, as we practice holding the frequency of Love more consistently, we become capable of creating new reality, moment-to-moment. Creativity becomes a way of creating life itself, of *thriving*.

2
ASK YOURSELF: WHAT IS LOVE?

Recently, I had to articulate to someone profoundly and singularly special to me, what I mean by Love with a capital L. And, here's how it came out spontaneously: Love is (given) when I reflect to another, his highest and best. And Love is (received) when I love and live up to the highest and best of myself that another reflects back to me. In this way,

Love is always a creative force that shapes and sculpts one to reveal one's highest and best self, returning one to the original purity of one's spirit, and thereby bringing one to communion with Spirit.

I have understood Love in its greatest depth because of two relationships book-ending a decade, which brought me closest to another at the level of soul rather than of personality, background, or other acquired or conditioned attributes. When you truly connect at the soul-level, the other person serves as a reflection of you – like a clear mirror. Just as any creation of yours is a reflection of you and thereby shapes you just as much as you shape it, so also is a soul relationship the ultimate playground for the transformation of you to your highest and best self. Just like in the practice of creativity, in such a relationship, you are Michelangelo and you are also David – at every turn, you are creating the other and you are being created by the other!

So, I offer here, some of my observations on Love, based on several years of (continuously transforming) revelations, practice, meditation, counseling and coaching.

LOVE IS AN INNER WAY OF BEING

Love is a way of being and therefore, also a way of acting in the world. It is not merely a bunch of good feelings, though these feelings are a natural and beautiful corollary to Love. Love is first an innate quality of oneself, independent of a relationship or situation or another person. Because it originates and emanates from within oneself, how much Love there is only depends on how much one's heart is open and willing to give *and* receive. As Marianne Williamson said in an interview with Oprah Winfrey, "The only thing lacking in any situation is what you are not giving it,"[9] and I would add, "not receiving from it." And as Benjamin Zander said in a TED Talk,[10] "Who am I being that (your) eyes are not shining?"

LOVE IS UNCONDITIONAL

When I first heard the term unconditional love, I wondered: What other kind of Love is there? Some have the perspective that there is no such thing as 'unconditional,' because in the end, even when we are being selfless it results in a good feeling in ourselves. Of course a selfless act makes oneself feel great! But outcome must not be conflated with intention. An act is selfless when its *intention* transcends one's own small, selfish needs and wants. That the act gives one joy is a happy by-product, and this outcome is not the underlying motivation for the action. The only motivation is the pure, free-of-want caring behind the action. Therefore, the unconditional nature of Love simply means that Love exists entirely free of attachment to outcome.

Another way to say it is that Love is based in detachment, rather than attachment, a word often mistakenly used interchangeably with love! Love is not based in ideas or assessments on what the other person should or shouldn't do, or whether the other person expresses their caring in this way or that, or whether the person deserves it, and so on. Such kinds of associations and conditions are essentially, attachment, and not Love. In this way, the unconditional nature of Love also means that it is unreasonable – it transcends reason.

---

[9] Find Williamson's interview on Oprah's Super Soul Sunday at: www.oprah.com/own-super-soul-sunday
[10] Watch: http://www.ted.com/talks/benjamin_zander_on_music_and_passion.html

LOVE IS 'PASSION WITH'

The feelings associated with Love's purest and truest form are compassion, enthusiasm, delight, inspiration, wonderment, awe, joy, gratitude, and peace. Feelings such as nervous excitement and suspense typically associated with romance, while seemingly enjoyable, are really lurking forms of fear – the absence of Love – because they are founded in the potential of loss.

In my first Vipassana meditation course in 2008, the teacher listed 'passion' in the problematic list of driving forces. I was stunned. How can I do anything without passion? Upon breaking silence at the end of eleven days and having a chance to speak to the teacher, I made my quiet enquiry. She answered gently, "In true Love you will feel mostly com-passion, that is, *passion with*." Although I didn't get her right away, I agreed to sit with this. In the several years since, I have repeatedly experienced such deep compassion in all my relationships, including romantic ones, that it has forever made this understanding a visceral part of me.

The experience of com-passion hit home fully when I experienced my vision and aspirations naturally and rapidly transform (– no, they did *not* become repressed or compromised –) each time my beloved preferred something different, and was uncomfortable fulfilling my aspirations of the moment. I found that loving him not only renders me *incapable* of wanting what he doesn't want, but it also inspires me to actively *invest* in what he does want! This is the experiential difference between passion and com-passion. I've now become passionate about what makes my beloved most comfortable and happy – I have *passion with* him!

LOVE IS RESPECT

It is often said that there's respect in Love. This suggests that respect is a nice-to-have aspect of Love. Once I moved into com-passion, however, I experienced that Love *is* respect. Because I am now invested in what my beloved wants, I'm always naturally honoring his wishes. I have unquestioning faith that there is some larger, cosmic truth and perfection in his preference of the moment, which necessarily includes my highest and best interests as well, even if I cannot always or immediately see how. All this amounts to a deep, deep respect; in fact, it is an experience of sheer reverence. So, in this way, Love *is* respect. And when respect is lacking – any degree of condescension or contempt or "I know better"[11] and so on – what's left is not Love; it is merely attachment.

LOVE GROWS IN CONFLICT

The central idea that *I am invested in what he wants* has led me to experience how Love actually grows in conflict. First, respect and faith enable me to know that conflict is going to reveal something beneficial for me, so my loved one and I are always on the same side even if conflict makes it appear as though we're on opposite ones. Next, conflict is essentially a mismatch of aspirations (and the assumptions, beliefs, values, etc. that underlie those aspirations). So, whenever conflict comes up, the compassion, faith and respect in my Love make it impossible for me to remain attached to my aspirations. I am forced to examine them, or at least sit with them, as well as with the beliefs and values underlying them. With stillness and detachment, invariably, I

---

[11] The famous relationship researchers, the Gottmans of University of Washington, have found that of the four "Horsemen of Apocalypse," contempt alone can be a strong predictor of divorce! Read: http://isoulseek.com/sitebranches/relationskills/articles/6signs.pdf

am shown how the new path opening up due to the 'No' is guiding me toward some bigger and better possibility. The 'No' leads to a big 'Yes'! When I am shown this, the awe, delight, enthusiasm and gratitude that come with it are indescribable. Instantly, Love grows and deepens.

LOVE IS A POSITIVE SUM GAME

It follows from many of the previous observations that Love is a positive sum game; meaning, that it is always good for others *and* oneself. So, what if someone or something is toxic? Then the unconditionality of Love leads me to lovingly separate (in the material plane) from that person, because I'm able to say, "Since I love her unconditionally, I must love her without expecting her to change for me. And because she's toxic right now, the only way forward at this moment is to give her the space to follow her path independent of me." This allows my loved one to grow at her own pace, and also allows me to move forward and grow in healthy ways as well, without ever lessening any of the Love. To the contrary, such detachment allows true Love to keep growing even in physical absence! In this way, Love is good for everyone involved. It's always a positive sum game.

LOVE IS LIGHT

Love is Light, and I mean this in both senses – illumination and humor! True Love is a high vibration, and not only results in an awakened state but also a light-hearted one, always providing perspective and joy, and lots of room for silliness and returning to our original, childlike selves. (Notice I didn't say 'childish'!) There's something I like to call the 'cosmic laugh' – the kind of laughter that bursts forth when one has so much perspective that one sees the humor in all of life, in every situation, no matter how tough and even painful it may be in the functional or operational sense. Love keeps us constantly connected with that cosmic laugh, the ability to find humor and light-heartedness in all-that-is, *just the way it is.*

LOVE IS A CONNECTION WITH ONESELF

Because Love makes one so aware of oneself – one's feelings, beliefs, values, aspirations, conflict areas, and so on – it is essentially a deep connection with oneself. On the inside, it acts as a sculpting agent that inspires and compels one to become one's highest and best self, connect with one's soul purpose, and serve the world with it. On the outside, Love radiates from within, flows outward, grows and transforms from the interactions with the external world, and then returns to oneself with priceless riches, only to continuously expand one's capacity for Love.

LOVE IS CREATIVE AND GENERATIVE

Because it is a connection to and an expansion of oneself, Love becomes deeply connected to one's soul purpose in the world, and to one's creativity. It becomes the generative power behind all one's actions. It makes one expansive and creative, liberating one from the boxes and limitations we frequently place ourselves in, and locating one, instead, always in the realm of limitless possibility. Now Love becomes the Muse for all creation. Eventually, like a tree emitting oxygen as a natural, effortless outcome of its being on the planet, one becomes a radiant source of Love and healing simply by one's being, from which all those near and afar can tangibly benefit.

LOVE IS DISCIPLINE

Love is (a) discipline. While spontaneity is certainly very much part of Love's expression, Love guides us to be centered, tenacious, committed, and always in integrity. This Love is fierce – there is no room for fooling oneself or others. It is an internal fire test, demanding a constant examination of ourselves and causing the sloughing off of anything that isn't authentic in the moment, which can sometimes be an incredibly uncomfortable process. This doesn't mean Love isn't gentle and joyful, though. Because it is deeply compassionate, what it always does is gently but firmly keeps us in the truth of ourselves. It rarely allows us to go astray from our inner calling and true way of being, and if we momentarily forget or lose our way, it quickly and efficiently shows us the way home.

LOVE IS *ALWAYS* MUTUAL!

And here's the grand finale, the big but simple secret: Love is *always* mutual! How many times have you found yourself wondering if your Love is returned, reciprocated, mutual? (Of course, in the very moment that you catch yourself wondering, you've already fallen out of true Love and into attachment!) Here's the amazing, awe-inspiring insight with which I've been blown away. By virtue of being all the things that it is, true Love, by definition, is *always and necessarily* mutual. When one unerringly holds the quality and frequency of Love, it has absolutely no way but to become the quality and frequency of all one's interactions, at the other end of which, are the persons in question. Like the other prong of a tuning fork, because the other is an integral part of this truly loving interaction, she is bound to hold the same frequency as you are emanating. Regardless of how she acts in the material realm, if you are holding true Love, you can be absolutely, unequivocally certain that she is with you in Love!

REFLECTIONS

1   Do you find that Love is innate to your way of being? Is your heart completely open and willing to give as well as receive?

2   What does unconditional Love mean to you? Do you see yourself practicing loving detachment due to which you are able to care more?

3   Are you in 'passion with' the one(s) you Love? Is deep respect the foundation of all your loving relationships?

4   Can you think of ways you can grow Love through conflict? How can you practice stillness and detachment to see new and bigger possibilities? Are you able to create story maps for conflict situations?

5   Do you see that Love must always first be good for *you*? Can you think of ways in which your loved one(s) and you can both have the space to transform at your own unique paces?

6   Can you feel the lightness in your relationship(s)? Is there something weighing on you right now? Is there room to find possibility by using humor and lightness?

7   How are you connecting with and transforming yourself as you practice Love? Is your Love fueling your creativity? Is Love a discipline for you?

3

TRANSMUTE UNDERLYING BELIEFS FROM FEAR TO LOVE

The most powerful way to transmute fear into Love is to bring Presence to our ingrained, underlying beliefs created by fear, which in turn generate unconscious and reactive assumptions, expectations, perceptions and feelings, keeping us trapped in a loop of fear.

Working within myself in a deepening creative and spiritual awakening, and coaching or witnessing others through their creative and spiritual paths, I've discovered that besides a chronically attachment-based concept of love, there are some key topical areas in which our beliefs have the greatest stronghold, and therefore, place the largest limitations on our creativity. These are our beliefs around the constructs of justice, life values, time, self, money, and truth. If we can gently bring Presence to our beliefs in these areas, with Love, lightness and humor, we can make quantum leaps in our creativity!

JUSTICE
Move beyond right-and-wrong into responsibility

If I could inspire you to do just *one* thing to unlock your true creativity, I'd ask you, lovingly, to get off your soapbox about the terrible state of the world!

True creativity comes from Love, from the heart and the soul, which don't critically analyze, judge or label. The soul *imagines*. It *envisions*. It *dreams*. And it does these things *just because*, to serve the Muse. While the soul does recognize problems and needs in the world, it doesn't become too attached to them. In the process of serving the Muse, its joyful creations naturally and organically meet needs, solve problems and serve the world positively. Serving the Muse is our responsibility and the only true morality – to simply be and create in integrity with the divine gift of imagination and potential we've each been given. Sufi saint Jalaluddin Rumi said,

> "Out beyond ideas of wrongdoing
> and rightdoing there is a field.
> I'll meet you there.
> When the soul lies down in that grass
> the world is too full to talk about."

And spiritual teacher Derek Rydall said in a recent podcast from the Fall 2012 series of *Healing with the Masters*:[12]

> "What is trying to emerge through me? Who am I really and why am I alive? My prayer for the longest time has been, God, more than I want to change, fix, heal or manipulate anything or anyone, I want to wake up – to who and what I really am and why I am alive. More than I want to control, manipulate and fix anything, I want to wake up – to the truth that makes me free. I want to see with divine eyes; I want to know with the heart of God; I want to feel with the soul of Spirit. I want to see what is really here."

Concepts of right and wrong, justice, privilege and equity are mental constructs, and are productive to a reasonable extent for guiding a thoughtful and intellectually mature existence. When you're stopped peacefully at a red

---

[12] See: http://www.healingwiththemasters.com/

light and someone hits you from the back, sure, you may pull over and follow through with insurance exchange information and other legal requirements for an appropriate resolution. If someone does egregious wrong unto you or a loved one, yes, you may choose to take legal recourse. And issues of social injustice may also cause you moral outrage and thereby inspire action. But none of these courses of action need be based in anger, bitterness, or more subtly, an entrenched identification of oneself as right, and the other as wrong. These courses of corrective action may be loving ways of balancing a system that has become out of balance, but they need not be reactionary or self-righteous.

When not grounded in Love, the concepts of right and wrong, justice and equity become founded in lack, in the potentially self-aggrandizing idea of bettering a deficiency, and therefore, by definition, based in some derivative of absence and separateness. Taken to an extreme, these concepts can turn into ingrained beliefs like, "The world is an unfair place," "There is so much injustice and inequity everywhere," and so on. Stemming from this, a related illusory belief about self is also created. It is usually some variant of the rather burdensome, "I am here to make a difference by righting wrongs." Now we begin to create meaning for our existences in lack as well!

Alarmist speech and obsession with the latest social, political or environmental issue, and founding your personal cause in correcting an egregious 'wrong' against somebody or something, only add to your (and the collective consciousness') mental baggage. Worse still, they can make you chronically sad, angry, bitter and reactionary, and these states prevent creativity from flowing and miracles from occurring through you. You might become a bristling activist with considerable momentum in fighting your cause, but you won't do much to unlock and liberate the true creativity within you to transform or *create* the world as a thriving place.

The belief in self-righteous justice is something most of us find very hard to transform from fear to Love because it is so ingrained in everything we've been taught through generations of human existence. It seems only reasonable, and to detach from justice seems outright irresponsible and even outrageous to the rational mind. I remind you again of Einstein's exhortation that no problem can be solved with the same consciousness that created it. I invite you lovingly, to try detaching from ideas of right and wrong just for a few days, to experience the liberation and unfettered imagination that can flow from such unburdening. It becomes easy when you remember that all deviance from Love is, to begin with, an illusion in material reality. In the spiritual plane – the space of pure creativity – nothing is ever wrong or lacking to begin with. As Marianne Williamson writes in *The Law of Divine Compensation*,

"Every loving thing that ever happened to you was real, and everything else was an illusion."

This doesn't in the least mean that it didn't happen, but it means that it happened only in the illusory, material plane of fear, lack and absence. When you leap from fear to Love and begin *creating* the world of your dreams rather than *correcting* the one you presently encounter, you assume your true responsibility to this world. As Williamson reminds us, in so doing you're not looking away from problems, but looking *through* them, to see beyond into a realm of limitless possibility. So, like the Wright Brothers imagining an airplane or John F. Kennedy imagining a man on the moon, look up into the sky with an open heart and imagination, and ask yourself "What if?"... and just dream. Then, listen for the whispers that guide you, and *then* act! When you act in this way, you've begun to create.

REFLECTIONS

1   Can you think of a situation in the world that you feel very strongly about and would like to do whatever it takes to 'right the wrong'?

2   Can you bring Presence to your thoughts and find ways to look beyond the wrongness? What are some loving and creative ways in which you can practice bringing about transformation in your own life, associated with this situation? Are you able to found these in what you want to see happen rather than what 'shouldn't' happen?

TIME [1]
Recognize that past and future exist only in our minds

The concept of linear time is another major belief to dismantle, or at least begin to pry loose, in order to unlock one's pure creativity. While linear time is experienced within material reality and can be leveraged successfully within it, at the level of the soul, which transcends physicality, I sense that there is neither space, nor time. This is what intensely creative people or athletes (or kids!) mean when they talk about transcendental experiences of "being in the zone," and how "time stops still."

The immense power of true creativity is unleashed when we can let go of the construct of time progressing linearly from the past to the present and then on to the future, and surrender instead, to nothing but the 'eternal Now,' as Eckhart Tolle terms it. In *The Law of Divine Compensation* Marianne Williamson writes,

"Every single moment, every single holy instant, the universe is ready to begin again. The only time God intersects with linear time is in the present moment."

In allowing ourselves to slow down, always be present in the Now, and simply experience time as cycles of day and night, the moon phases, the four seasons, and so on, the transcendental experience of *no-time* opens up. If the sun rose yesterday and once again this morning, and will do so again tomorrow, then is there a past? Or a future? The only thing there is, is a series of stories to fill up our minds between the various sunrises, which are simply repeat points of Now! We're able to see that past and future are created solely in the mind, in the Now.

Here's a fun thought experiment to explore this understanding further. I often contemplate the many stars we see in the night sky. As we well know, many of them *physically* do not exist right now – they have already perished. But we are seeing their light on Earth right now, because light has taken that much 'time' to travel to us! But if we're seeing their light right now, then they exist now in some form, at least as the waves they emitted, correct? This means that we're getting a glimpse of the past in the present! Now extend this thought and imagine that we – humanity and our Earth – have already perished, and some species is watching our 'light' from their vantage point in the future. Which means, this future possibility *also* exists right now. It follows, then, that both past and future 'exist' in the Now!

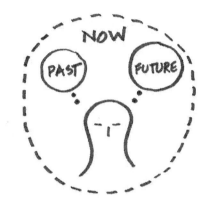

If the metaphysical discussion of time doesn't connect with you, simply think about life itself. Although we have conformed to linear time in our educational and professional systems, writing up resumes to indicate a perfectly linear chronology of events in our lives, has life really ever shown up in that way for you? For most of us, life is an organic and rather chaotic process, and through its non-linearity, cyclical patterns, and sometimes inexplicable quantum leaps, we find ourselves in interesting places we couldn't have planned for or foreseen in a linear way.

Several things are liberated when we see time as one conflated point of Now rather than a line of past-present-future. Rapidly, we drop our attachments created by baggage from the past and anxiety about the future. We stop constraining our creativity in terms of reactions to the past and to the potential future – solving for problems rooted in the past and for those that we portend to be significant in the future. We stop thinking limiting thoughts like, "But this has never been done before," or, "This will never fly."

Instead, when we become completely present in the Now, we know that in this moment, anything can be created from nothing by just seeing it freely in the imagination's eye and allowing creative action to flow through us. We see that both past and future are created in the Now, depending on how we choose to see them and story-tell about them, which also means that it is within our creative power to *transform* them! Anything becomes possible, and we step into our full creative potential.

As with the belief in right and wrong, attachment to linear time is challenging for many of us to relinquish, mostly because we would have to give up our idea that what "happened to us," determines where we are now, and where we are headed. We would have to accept instead, the awe-inspiring responsibility and power to create just about anything from nothing, in the Now, acting like an imaginal cell!

TIME [2]
Spot the wormholes for quantum leaps!

A belief related to the construct of linear time is that everything is a 'journey'! How often do we hear it said that "Life is a journey"? Or, things like, "That takes a long time to happen," or, "It's a process," and so on. These terms inherently imply linearity, sequence, durations and milestones for time.

I'm not denying process. Again, in material reality, things take time and yes, there's a process. But at the transcendental level of no-time, at which our souls create, even the mere thought-seed of creation is instantaneously correlated to an effect in the Universe. And this power to create instantaneously is *always already available*. It is simply a choice. The tangible, physical manifestation in material reality might appear to require linear time or process, but the spiritual act of creation and its correlated outcome exist in pure synchronicity, in no-time. There is nowhere to go and no other place to reach, other than where one *already is*. There is no linear journey or process; all success is available right here, right now, should we truly choose it!

This idea is important to grasp in order to unlock full creative potential, because we tend to disguise fear and resistance by hiding behind the workings of process, often running busily on a treadmill, headed nowhere. Add this notion of process to our constructs and beliefs about 'hard work' – always an arduous, upward climb – and we can become chronically plagued with hiding and excuse-making, refusing to make the simple, easy leaps available to us.

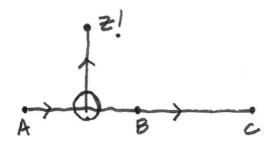

When we open ourselves to the mysterious possibilities of no-time, we are liberated from sequence, linearity, durations and milestones. We begin to spot the wormholes, and can ride them joyfully to make quantum jumps from one possibility state to another, often in a completely unrelated, non-sequitur way, like transforming from a goop-cell to an imaginal cell! Suddenly, with nothing but turning on the switch of choice, a brand new career emerges without the process of accumulating 'years of experience,' cancer unexpectedly goes into remission, a long-lost friend reappears from the blue, and so on. The cosmic power of Spirit is channeled to help you co-create with its ability for instantaneous correlation, simultaneity and synchronicity.

When I gently suggest to someone that things don't need to be such a process or journey, I often meet tremendous, fierce, and sometimes even angry resistance. This is because it threatens to negate or devalue experience accumulated through physical age and time, or to expose hidden excuses. It all comes back to the fear of accepting full responsibility for one's immense creative power.

REFLECTIONS

1   Think of a situation in which you are feeling stuck or fearful based on past experience and/or uncertainty about the future. Write down your past story that is generating the fear and your future story that is causing the worry. Now strike them out and simply write your present story as is, without using any language from your past or future stories. Do you see possibility in the new story? Do you see that the past and future are only as you tell it?

2   Is there a possibility for yourself that you periodically glimpse in your vision, but that appears like a far-removed dream both in terms of time and resources? Are beliefs like "But, how can I change it so easily or quickly?" holding you back? Can you imagine simply dropping the obstacles in your head and making a leap?

VALUES [1]
Integrate opposing values

One of the biggest things that kept me stuck in status quo for a long, long time was the subconscious belief in opposing values. An example is my past belief that for a woman, an illustrious and powerful career, and a deeply, mutually caring and fulfilling relationship with a male partner are necessarily at odds. Or that being as wildly creative as I'd like to be, and enjoying financial prosperity, or even be loved and accepted by my friends and family, are in conflict. Or that having financial success and having adequate (alone) time for my spiritual be-ing practice, are at odds. This idea of competing values is essentially based in the illusory belief in duality – that certain things are opposing and mutually exclusive, so I am forced to choose one or the other.

Once one is aware of the tricks of fear, it's easy to see how this is a scam of the ego! In being whole and abundant Love is a positive sum game, which means that it never forces one to choose between two things. Love allows for integration. So, the way to shine Love on to this belief in duality or mutual exclusiveness is to simply integrate the opposing values, to realize that one value can actually not just allow for the other, but even synergistically expand and empower it! Even in the context of business, entrepreneurship and leadership, Roger Martin's entire thesis in his brilliant book, *The Opposable Mind,* is that this ability for integrative thinking is the distinguishing quality of successful leaders.

In my case, some of the examples I cited earlier, transformed in this way when I integrated seemingly opposing beliefs. I saw that the more illustrious and genuinely powerful a career I enable, the higher my chances of having a deeply, mutually caring and fulfilling relationship with a male partner, and conversely, the more I invest in such a relationship, the better my career! Similarly, the more chances I take with my creativity, the better my financial success can be, and the more financial success I have, the more I can continue to be creative as well as have (alone) time for my spiritual be-ing. And I can also be loved and accepted by my friends and family under all these circumstances!

By integrating these seemingly opposing and competing values, I was able to transcend the fearful trap of ego and status quo. This belief is challenging to transform because straightforward rational and analytical thinking don't show us how this integration is possible. One must transcend reason. Only faith and a deep awakening to Love make it possible.

VALUES [2]
Flip sequence and conditionality

A corollary to the beliefs in opposing values and in linear time, is the belief in a sequence to things, and further still, uni-directional conditionality in this sequence. How often do we hear, "When X happens I can do Y"? All the time! "When my children grow up and leave home, I'll pursue my music." "When I lose weight I'll buy that dress." "When my spouse is settled into her job, I'll change mine." "When my idea is fully formed and I have enough money saved up, I'll start my company."... And so on.

In each case, this belief in conditionality creates illusory obstacles to creative action by allowing us to pretend that one thing facilitates the other, and by obscuring the only obstacle there really ever is – fear. This belief also excludes the possibility of the reverse in conditionality! What if one could lose weight by buying that dress and being motivated to fit in it, make money from that new company one started, inspire the spouse to settle into her job by initiating change in one's own, and so on? I find that without exception, if 'Y' truly serves the Muse, then doing it *anyway* automatically makes 'X' happen as well! I have countless examples in my personal and creative life to support this claim, and many of the participants in the Creativity Workshops I coach have seen similar results.

The belief in sequence and conditionality is challenging to transform because it requires us to drop imaginary obstacles and again, make the leap of faith to take responsibility for our immense creative powers.

REFLECTIONS

1 Can you think of an example of two opposing values in your life which you have never questioned because your rational mind tells you there is no way for both to successfully happen together? Can you ignore your rational mind for a moment and explore the possibility of a new story wherein the two values could not only co-exist but even synergistically fuel each other?

2 Are you waiting for something particular to happen as a pre-condition to be able to do something you truly want? What would really happen if you did what you want to, anyway? Is it possible that what you are waiting on will happen automatically? Is it even important for it to happen anymore?

SELF [1]
Question the construct of humility

One of the most insidious self-limiting beliefs is the false construct of humility. *What?* you ask!

By the false construct of humility, I'm referring to playing small and refusing to step into one's immense creative potential. We think we're being humble when we claim that we're not as talented as the other, or that our situation limits us, or say how we prefer to be invisible or behind-the-scenes because that's the equivalent of being humble, or when we reject appreciation or acknowledgment, or state how we don't deserve something, and so on. Unfortunately, this is nothing but a sham, another behavior motivated by fear, ego and resistance. It is a construct to hide safely behind so we don't have to take on the responsibility for being our highest selves, and the possible failure associated with that awesome endeavor.

True humility spontaneously arises from loving and owning one's immense creative power, which brings us face-to-face with Spirit. *Then* we are humble, because we are completely floored with gratitude for our awesomeness, by our ability to channel Spirit's power of Creation. We are in grateful acceptance of Spirit's immense gift, and we step up to the responsibility placed on us. In doing so, we honor and we love and we are truly and utterly humbled. We wake up the next day and want to serve all over again.

These oft-repeated, powerful lines from Marianne Williamson's classic bestseller *A Return to Love*, illustrate what I am saying better than anything else:

"Our deepest fear is not that we are inadequate. Our deepest fear is that we are powerful beyond measure. It is our light, not our darkness that most frightens us. We ask ourselves, Who am I to be brilliant, gorgeous, talented, fabulous? Actually, who are you not to be? You are a child of God. Your playing small does not serve the world. There is nothing enlightened about shrinking so that other people won't feel insecure around you. We are all meant to shine, as children do. We were born to make manifest the glory of God that is within us. It's not just in some of us; it's in everyone. And as we let our own light shine, we unconsciously give other people permission to do the same. As we are liberated from our own fear, our presence automatically liberates others."

Trust me, it is in this glorious shining of your highest self, in liberation from fear, in enabling others to shine and be liberated as well, that *true* humility lies!

SELF [2]
Let the Imposter Syndrome show you the way

When we *do* make the leap and step into our fuller creative potential, a belief that can suddenly show up to nag us is that we're a total fake, an imposter! We're actually not good enough to be doing what we're doing or being the way we're being. Constantly, we are hounded by the strange idea that the 'talent police' is going to expose and arrest us any moment. One little mistake and our big fraud will be revealed! Do this feeling and mental chatter sound familiar to you?

It was in my late twenties that I first learned about the Imposter Syndrome, something that I had experienced most of my life as a multi-talented and versatile person, and something that apparently many exceptional creators and risk-taking entrepreneurs feel at some point in their lives – this constant running from the talent police in fear of exposure. The Imposter Syndrome is a clever disguise of the ego; it is the ego chattering when we hear that we're not good enough and are going to be caught and exposed at any moment.

One day it occurred to me that I could use this rather annoying voice to my advantage, rather than be thwarted by it! Every time I felt like a fake and an imposter, I knew it was a sign that I was stepping out of my comfort zone and into creative potential, that I was taking a risk worth taking, and that I was on the edge of a quantum leap. I just had to leap and the new net would appear. Soon I'd connect with more imaginal cells, and the new playground and paradigm would become available for play. With practice, I would *become* who I have set out to be – who I've created – even if it feels fake at this moment. So, I began to allow the Impostor Syndrome to guide me on the creative path. The louder it screamed, the stronger my resolve became to proceed anyway!

So, rather than confronting or deconstructing the nagging belief that you aren't good enough, I suggest simply taking the presence and voice of the Imposter Syndrome as the very proof that you're on the right track. *Because* you're afraid of exposure, go for it!

REFLECTIONS

1   Do you find yourself hanging back and playing small because you believe that being habitually self-effacing is being humble? Do you judge others as self-promoting or envy them when they are fully expressing their gifts?

2   Think of a time you've felt like an imposter (you could have told this to yourself or someone else could have told you). Did it give you an easy way out of committing to something you wanted to do but were afraid of doing? What if you flipped things around, and took it as a sign to move right ahead?

MONEY [1]
Recognize your financial health as a state of mind

Money is another huge area in which limiting beliefs are carried, and these beliefs greatly block our creative potential. If you think about it, the most typical excuse that is offered for not doing something is either, "I don't have the time," or, "I don't have the money." It's easy to spot the fear-driven mindset latent in this condition when you observe that, most frequently, when we have the time we don't have the money, but when we have the money we suddenly don't have the time anymore!

Financial health is a state of mind, not the state of your bank balance! This state of mind – or *money thermostat* as I sometimes like to call it – which regulates the flow of money in and out of our lives, is determined by several money-related beliefs that we pick up through the conditioning in our upbringing or from the extant collective consciousness, formed and passed on through generations.

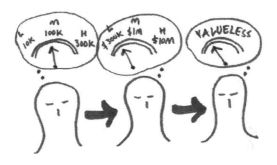

Some examples of money-related beliefs that create our thermostat (which in turn creates our financial health) are, "Money is dirty or impure," or "Wealthy people are dishonest or have taken advantage of others," or, "Truly great people don't need money," and so on. On the other side there are beliefs like, "I'm never going to have enough," "I can't afford the life I want," "Money is hard to make," and so on. Both sides of the coin are fear-based mental states fueled by feelings of guilt, greed, lack, or want.

When we replace these fear-based beliefs with ones based in Love, our thermostat is recreated, and money automatically and organically begins to flow. Try on beliefs like, "Prosperity is a pure reflection of my true nature of Love," "I always have enough," "I always have exactly what I need," "The world wishes to compensate me for the gifts I give it," "Money naturally flows through me," and so on.

MONEY [2]
See that money is Love energy!

The reason one's financial health is more a state of mind rather than the state of one's bank balance is that there is nothing physically 'real' about money. Think about it – what does that piece of paper mean? Or where does your bank-balance physically sit? As a little girl growing up in India, I used to imagine stacks of bills in a safe when my parents took me along to the bank, and I was stunned when I realized that the money they presumably had was simply an account sheet somewhere, and in those days it was manually maintained on paper! When the price of your property falls, where does the balance amount go? How is the value of a diamond intrinsically different from that of a tulip, which was once considered valuable enough to be used as currency?

We, as mortal humans, created money as a proxy, a middleman for the barter of goods, because at some point, I didn't want your apples in exchange for my firewood anymore. I wanted to pass on your apples to someone else, and I was alright with your doing the same with my firewood, so you and I created a proxy symbol to enable this trade, assigning a (largely arbitrary) value to apples and firewood, based on the situation and context, and mutual assessment of need. Then, suddenly, I saw the opportunity to pass on your apples for...a profit! I could now make more of that shiny stuff because the poor guy in the neighboring tribe desperately wanted apples, and was willing to do anything for them! What Nature gave to us freely, we converted into profit. As soon as we created the concepts of relative value and profit, we created something illusory, with no physical existence or meaning.

The only way to truly understand and relate to money, therefore, is as flow, as *energy*. It can be fear-based energy, embodying which we view and experience the world as a place of lack, and we are always left wanting. Or it can be Love-based energy, embodying which we view and experience the world as an abundant, resourceful and prosperous place. (This doesn't mean that we 'give' money to assuage underlying guilt, which is again a fear-based condition.) Once we become open to both giving and receiving this Love energy, invariably, the physical translation of this energetic flow manifests material prosperity as well.

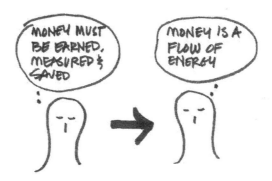

One simple shortcut for stepping into the flow of money as energy is to use the "X will happen when I do Y" trick. Instead of believing that you need enough money before you follow your calling and serve your Muse, try on the reverse – that serving the Muse will naturally allow money (or material abundance in some form) to flow to and through you. But never do this for the sole purpose of making money; do it for the Love and joy of it. Make a life before you make a living, and the livelihood will naturally follow. When you are acting in integrity with your highest creative potential, the Universe has the uncanny ability and generosity to give you exactly what you need, when you need it!

REFLECTIONS

1 Do you have a Love-based view of money? How does it feel to consider, "I always have exactly what I need"? And how about, "I have exactly as much as I believe I can have?"

2 Can you see money as a flow of energy? How does it feel to consider, "The more wealth I create to flow to me, the more will flow *through* me to others, and vice-versa"?

TRUTH [1]
Know your language as an act of creation

In the previous chapter we explored the construct of 'the truth,' and the idea that it's always a story. And we observed that which story we choose to tell is really up to us!

The significance of this choice is monumental. Our language is a powerful act of creation, and most of us are completely unaware of this. Or if we're aware, we haven't worked up the discipline to streamline our language. And by language, I don't mean just what we speak or write, but every thought we generate in our minds, which brings with it, its share of emotional and physical feelings. *Every* such thought is an act of creation. Actually, the wheels of creation begin to turn even before thought, at the level of intention. And we are sure to experience the outcomes of intention and thought in some form or another, whether we recognize them or not!

When we embody our true nature as Love and choose to tell the most creative, generative story, we become conscious creators of Truth with our language. Truth is no longer a function of past stories, but it is created in the Now, moment-to-moment, in our intentions, thoughts, and spoken language. And the secret to consciously using thought and language to create Truth moment-to-moment, is to always think and speak in terms of what you *envision* instead of what you 'don't want.' This is the essence of creative storytelling.

When we think or speak in terms of what we don't want, where is this 'don't want' coming from? It can only come from a reaction to the past, and a fear of the same thing repeating itself in the future, right? It is a comparative, preventive, surviving, fear-driven stance; it is neither based in Love, nor present in the Now! Take for example, the simple case of our desire to be on time to something. Somehow, most of us manage to say, "I don't want to be late!" rather than the more intentional, "I'd love to be on time." Or, consider the case of a close friend who was unhappy with his inability to have healthy, loving romantic relationships. When I asked him what he wants out of such a relationship, along with saying that he wants "someone smart, caring, independent and athletic," he began to also say things like, "Well, I really don't want to be held back or criticized;" "I don't want someone to be dependent on me;" "I don't want her to be emotionally volatile;" and so on. Each of these 'don't wants' is a reaction to the past.

And, here's the trickier thing – each of these 'don't wants' is also a creation! For each time we think or say 'don't want,' we're putting into motion this energy of absence, lack and deficiency, and attracting exactly that into our lives! This is because this is a re-action – like an action replay, it must re-enact itself! It reveals a lack or wound in our own selves that needs healing and completion, and Spirit continues to place those things in our experience so that we can heal from hurt to acceptance, and then beyond into Love and creativity. Spirit is always compassionate and generous, and will unfailingly give us exactly what we need for true soul-level transformation! If we don't recognize this and stay stuck in the fear-based loop, we'll continue to create exactly what we *don't want*, again and again.

When we focus our intention, thought and language on what we *do* want, we are creating in the Now. We are free of comparisons to the past and apprehensions of the future, and the sky is the limit on what we can imagine, intend, and say. I encourage myself and others to truly take this incredible creative power of language very seriously, and be aware and attentive at absolutely all times without exception. This includes when you're in the line at the grocery store, when someone cuts in front of you in traffic, when you're chatting casually with your mother on the phone...it is a constant, disciplined way of being.

Keep in mind that I'm not talking about 'positive thinking,' which has come to be an effort to sound all perky even when you're feeling low, merely masking negative feelings. What I'm talking about *does* acknowledge your feelings, allows them to flow through you like we've discussed before, which then reveals the blank canvas underneath, on to which anything can be painted. I'm speaking of embodying your true nature of Love, which gives you the faith to freely imagine and create Truth, moment-to-moment.

TRUTH [2]
Tell the short story with the long line

The mapping of story possibilities from which the most loving, generative one can be chosen almost invariably leads me to an idea so extraordinarily important that I cannot emphasize it enough. This is the idea of the short(est) story with the long(est) line.

As you may have guessed from the story mapping examples in the previous chapter, I've discovered that practicing this exercise organically leads us to choosing the shortest, simplest possible story. This is because, very quickly we realize that like a potent seed, the most creative story contains nothing but the essence in it; all else is just extra fluff that takes energy away from its potency to create!

While the chosen, creative story is simple, it's by no means an over-simplification. What also emerges along with the shortness and simplicity of the story is its 'long line' – the arc that communicates its overarching vision, which is far-reaching and sustainable over the long term. In *The Art of Possibility*, Ben Zander writes about the long line in classical music compositions, and how, often, when musicians playing in symphony lose sight of the long line and become over-focused on playing their own piece within the composition to perfection, they actually do a disservice to the *essential storyline* and intended message or vision of the composition! The long line of any creative product is its intention, its vision, its essential message – that which touches, moves and inspires others, and catalyzes transformation.

In the example previously discussed about the Creativity Workshop participant working with gemstones and Reiki, "I design healing" was her potent short story with a long line. It is short and potent through two components – in the creative action – design, and the intended benefit for humanity – healing. Its long line presents a powerful vision – the possibility for design to heal, and conversely, for healing to be designed! It has a long line also because it is unattached to any particular method, such as jewelry making, or gemstones, or Reiki. It allows the creator to begin her work through these current avenues, and transform over time to multiple other avenues, with no expiry date to her statement "I design healing"! Even so, it rings authentically true to her present occupation as a jewelry maker and Reiki practitioner, and to her attitude of service. Sheer genius!

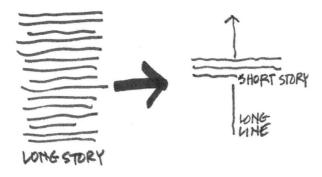

In the case of the personal example I had referenced regarding migraines, "I am healing" is the short story with a long line. The potent shortness of it is obvious, and the long line is a vision for my continuous healing, something that is miraculously always already available to our bodies. That all disease is actually a sign of being out of integrity and an opportunity to activate the choice to heal, is a powerful, creative idea. "I am healing" creates the possibility for healing and wellness for me and for all others, and it rings true forever so long as I can relinquish my attachment to a story of suffering.

I also love telling the story of my dear friend and entrepreneurial partner Shirin, a story I've told previously in my book *Thrive!* and in numerous coaching sessions and speeches. When she transitioned into founding *Flying Chickadee* with me, she often told the longer, reactive story about her journey when asked, "What are you doing these days?" at social gatherings and such. Then one day she heard herself saying, "I am the co-founder of a publishing platform for stories of courage, creativity and change." And she felt every cell in her body fire up with the electric energy of the short story with the long line!

Always telling the short(est) story with the long(est) line is a powerful, transformative, creative practice. It will completely transform your life!

REFLECTIONS

1   Pick a day and keep track of how many times you use "I don't want..." in your language. Can you think of ways to express the same thing beginning with "I want..."? Try it and see how you feel.

2   How would you tell the shortest story about your life? Does it have a long line, a vision? If not, can you re-write it to have the longest line within the shortest form?

4
EMPLOY LOVE AS THE CREATIVE FORCE

Along with shifting your beliefs, here are some actionable practices to directly access Love as the creative agent to sculpt you, your reality, and all your creative endeavors in the world.

REMEMBER YOU'RE THE CREATOR *AND* THE ACTOR

The very first thing participants do in the Creativity Workshops I coach, is practice becoming the neutral observer of any situation, and of themselves and others within it. Becoming the observer automatically connects us with the realization of being the creator, not merely the actor within the story that is unfolding.

In practicing this idea, the metaphor of theater or film works very well. While watching a film or play with a dramatic storyline, we might become emotionally and viscerally involved, yet most of us manage to remember that it is a play or film we're watching, and that it isn't 'really' happening. What if you considered that this is the case with your life as well? That what's happening in the material playground is not real, but a reflection of your creations? And what's even better in the case of your life, is that you're not just passively in the viewer's seat, but you're both the real-time playwright *and* the central actor within the story you are writing! It also follows that you've cast others into the roles of your own scripting. So you have the power to transform the story at least at two levels – of creator *and* actor.

The Creator-Actor practice always works wonders in the Creativity Workshops. When we see the story unfolding as our own creation, including the roles others are playing in it – villain, victim, hero – we begin to own our true creative power. We understand our lives as a reflection of our intentions and imaginations, become open to all possibility, and realize that the only thing lacking in the story is what we're withholding from it. We recognize that people who are playing not-so-great roles are also serving a purpose within our story – they may be wrong within its adopted moral frameworks, but they are creatively (and spiritually) correct, because they *fit* the story we've been creating! And if they don't fit anymore, we're free to re-script their roles or change the casting. Best of all, we realize that it is in our hands, what role *we* play within our own screenplay, as well as *how* we play it!

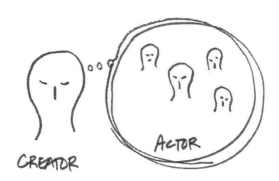

Besides the tremendous liberation and power this exercise provides, it also invariably invokes great humor, lightheartedness and playfulness within everyone who participates, expanding and elevating the energy in their beings. Even if people are complaining about something serious, they learn to talk about it in terms of roles they have cast or stories they have written, which means they take responsibility. Suddenly, a management consultant in a world-famous corporation owns up about an irritating manager, "I've cast Mr. X as my villain." The mom of a special needs child proposes that she can play the role of humorist in an upcoming parent-teacher's meeting. People become creative, funny and powerful. Suddenly, it is all up to us and us alone!

REFLECTIONS

1   Think about a life situation that has been causing you unrest. Step back and observe it as if it were a play scripted by someone. Do you see the different roles various people are playing, including you?

2   Now consider that you are the creator of this play in the first place, and you are the one who cast all the actors in their roles! Can you see how you might re-script the play? Might this re-cast the actors including yourself, or even eliminate some roles? How does that make you feel?

3   Every day, spend some moments being the creator of your situation or experience rather than merely the actor in it. Practice this regularly so that spontaneously jumping into your creator role becomes possible in all your life experiences.

KEEP YOUR HEART OPEN, LOVING AND FORGIVING

Keeping your heart open, loving and forgiving essentially means holding unerring faith and gratitude, leading life with the assumption that the world is a good place, full of possibility. It means expecting to be surprised pleasantly. It means assuming the best intentions in others and in all situations. It means knowing that those who show up in your path are in some way or another, reflections of you and your storytelling – either your shadow side or your light side – here to play a role in your screenplay, to reveal something. So, without characterizing anything as good or bad, you're able to respond with gratitude: "Thank you for showing me the way."

I find that in this way, each person, situation or circumstance becomes an ally in my path, in the story I've written. They either assist me, or block me because I need to take the other fork, or temporarily take me 'off course' because I need some additional information or experience, and so on. Most importantly, they reflect and reveal the ways in which I must re-write my story! So I respond with compassion, kindness, gentleness and gratitude, no matter what.

A significant nuance in this way of holding Love and faith is that it transcends acceptance. It's one thing to say that I accept the obstacles in my life and recognize how they teach me something. This is the level of compassionate reason. It's quite another thing to know in every cell of my being, that there is no obstacle to begin with! That what appears to be an obstacle is merely an illusory reflection in the material playground, a temporary condition here to reveal something. This is the level of Love, which transcends reason. It is the access to pure awareness, from which all creation is possible. Like humor and playfulness, this level of faith and gratitude feels expansive in your body. It opens you to possibility, to more of the same goodness coming your way. And, angels emerge from the woodwork to become agents in the service of your soul's endeavors!

BECOME KARMA NEUTRAL

I often smile thinking that more important than being carbon neutral on this planet, is to be karma neutral!

This practice explores the previous one of keeping your heart open and forgiving, to greater nuance. Karma, in Sanskrit, literally means the verb 'to do.' So it has come to connote action that generates a reaction, easily as much a principle of physics as of metaphysics. Rarely are two things considered though. The first thing is that karma is actually born at the level of intention, of thought. Even before action is taken, you are generating karma when you intend, think or feel something in a certain direction. Second, every single time we receive something pleasant or unpleasant in our path, we are actually receiving the karmic outcome of past intention, thought or action, whether individually or collectively.

This moment is a tremendous gift, if we can transcend the attachment to being right. In this moment of Now, we are gifted the incredibly creative opportunity to respond to the event in a way that generates no more karma! If I am able to simply say, "Thank you for this outcome of my / our past intention, thought or action," and thereby respond to everything, good or bad, with neutrality and gratitude, I generate no more karma. The accounts are closed. I become karma neutral, an incredibly powerful place of creativity because, again, the blank canvas with all possibility opens up. There is no more re-action (karma) in our lives, and only pure creation!

REFLECTIONS

1   Each time you find yourself approaching something with the attitude of "It's a problem unless proven otherwise," or "Uh-oh, I've seen this before," can you consider flipping your position to one of unerring faith?

2   Pick a day to explore what happens when you respond with gentleness, neutrality and gratitude to each turn of events. Feel the feeling in your heart. At the end of the day, make a list of ten things you are grateful for from that day.

3   When someone or something appears to be blocking your path, make a list of all the possible ways in which this can reveal something beneficial to you, or provide you with a welcome break, or redirect your story in a creative direction.

EXERCISE IMAGINATION AND EXPLORE POSSIBILITY

Anything you do to exercise your imagination and explore possibility will – without fail – access Love. This could be in a life situation like a broken down vehicle or financial crisis, in relational aspects such as raising your child, relating with your mother or spouse, or working with your colleague or boss, or in projects such as writing poetry, working on a new entrepreneurial venture, or organizing action around a purpose.

You will notice that exercising imagination and exploring possibility feel a certain way in your body. Your brain will function differently, your heart will beat differently, your chest and breathing will expand, you'll feel joy course through your body. This is a state of expansion – a sign of being in the frequency of Love – whereas the state of fear is one of physical contraction. No matter what it is you do, the moment you find an avenue to exercise imagination and explore possibility, you have moved into Love because fear cannot exist in the act of imagining possibility. And if you do this along with others in a co-creative group, you multiply the power of this practice exponentially.

LEAP HARD AND OFTEN IN INTEGRITY WITH YOUR INNER TRUTH

Exploring possibility will often reveal our inner truth of the moment. Getting access to our inner truth can be hard for some of us, because it requires a strong and unmediated connection to our intuition, to Love, and many of us are stuck spinning wheels in our perpetually reasoning intellects, often a vehicle of the ego. For many of us who do gain access to our inner truth, our real block is in fully acknowledging it, accepting it, and acting in integrity with it. We hide away from what we already know, and if we see it, we refuse to act on it or find very logical sounding reasons to postpone acting on it. And if we do act on it, we might do so cautiously, guardedly, suspiciously...constantly second-guessing ourselves. That's *not* leaping!

Leaping is an act of utter and unquestioning faith once the inner truth is revealed. So when I say, "Leap hard and often in integrity with your inner truth," I mean LEAP! No asking advice from others, no weighing pros and cons, no making spreadsheets for evaluation, no looking in the rearview mirror, no looking for a place to land...*just leap!*

Faith is an incredibly powerful energy frequency to hold. Again, the feeling in your body will be one of expansion, of taking flight. Leaping with faith often feels light and airy, like floating free of baggage and material limitations. Like in the movie *Inception*, you'll find that there's always a leap within a leap, with no real landing ground in sight. A light safety net will reveal itself as soon as you leap, to temporarily cradle you, until...you leap again!

FOLLOW THROUGH WITH ACTION

Next, take creative action in the direction of opportunities revealed as a result of taking the leap of faith. Positive, creative action is another immensely powerful vibrational frequency to embody. This means taking action daily – no matter what – write, paint, sing, dance, meditate, exercise, build, connect, simulate, solve equations, run experiments...whatever is applicable for your creative endeavor.

When fear knocks on the door with questions like "But what if it doesn't work?," "What if nobody buys it?" "What if she hates me for this?" and so on, allow yourself to go to that dark place of failure, and shine the light of Love on it, using gratitude and faith. Accept yourself as the failed human being you will be should your fearful "What if" indeed come true. Let the fearful feelings surface and allow them to pass through and clear as we explored in the previous chapter. Allow Love to wash them away! Soon, you'll find that maintaining faith is easy.

Creative action also feels incredibly expansive in the body. Think of the high of delivering a great speech, making a piece of woodwork, solving that equation in a fit of imagination, running the race of your life, and so on. In that moment that time stops still and you forget all else, your body is holding a high vibration. Generating that feeling again and again through creative action will keep you in the frequency of Love.

RELINQUISH ATTACHMENT TO OUTCOMES

This is the final step in allowing miracles into our lives, and the one most of us find the most challenging – detachment. Detachment means lovingly relinquishing attachment to outcome. It means shifting from expectation or resistance to being in unconditional, gentle acceptance. It means shifting from the mode of pursuit to a mode of *receiving* what channels through organically. Often what channels through is exactly what we need or asked for, but because we're attached to a particular form or timing we've envisioned, we're unable to recognize the gifts coming our way in a different form or at an unexpected time!

It helps to know that exactly what I've asked for or truly need in my life will *always* come my way – just perhaps in a different form or timing than I can predict or control. So, I must simply serve my calling of the moment with an open heart and without question. And I practice expanding my awareness for recognizing the gifts that are naturally coming my way so that I can receive them with the openness, respect and gratitude they merit, instead of trying to predict or control outcomes.

Letting go of outcomes takes a huge burden off our minds and bodies, and makes us feel lighthearted. Whenever you experience this feeling, it is a sign of having successfully elevated your frequency toward that of Love.

REFLECTIONS

1 Close your eyes and take a metaphorical leap with something you are holding yourself back on. How do you feel? What are you really afraid of? Are the fears real? Can you make the leap anyway, trusting that the Universe has the safety net to cradle you until you are ready to jump again? How does the leap feel now?

2 Take any one dream and take one small action toward it every single day no matter what, instead of thinking you have to do something big to serve the dream. See what happens.

3 What is the outcome you are hoping to achieve with either the big leap or the small actions? What if you were to completely let that go, and take action just to feel the high of leaping or taking action? Does that make your leap feel lighter and easier?

5
SING YOUR HIGHEST AND BEST MELODY!

By now you have a good sense that being in your original nature of Love involves a shift in your *energy* frequency. Sometimes, I explain this by using the analogy of music. What tune are you humming? Are you singing the melody you want to hear echoed back to you? Is it at the highest, best and richest frequency you can sing?

Apart from the practices of shifting into Love discussed in the previous section, other practices such as meditation and contemplation raise your energy frequency, as do moderate exercise, yoga, Qi gong and Reiki. The company of elevated spirits, fun and laughter, high quality sleep, healthy physical touch, classical music, and good foods prepared with care, are all simple agents for raising one's energy frequency. And the most fundamental of all avenues for raising our energy frequency is the very life-force flowing through us – our breath. There's no way to breathe consciously and be in a depressed energy frequency. So, breathe, let go, and sing your soul's melody!

While clearing our feelings, and transmuting fear-based mental beliefs to Love-inspired ones can do a lot to shift us into Love, the actual shift occurs in a mysterious, non-mental, non-linear way. It happens at the subtler level of energy, requiring a leap in the frequency of vibration that we hold, embody and radiate into the world.

I have an inkling that you could even do nothing at all to change your fear-based mental beliefs, but if by some miraculous, divine intervention of Spirit the frequency of energy vibrations you hold were to make a quantum leap, you would suddenly be in your true nature of Love, stumbling upon your full creative powers. For some this can happen in an instant as mundane as boarding a train with sliding doors, or something more extraordinary such as a spectacular experience in nature, or even momentarily facing death. Suddenly, there you are, in the energy of Love. And when you simply sing the highest melody of your soul – hold your highest frequency – the Universe has no other choice but to resonate with you, join you in harmony, and make music together!

This is actually what happens in a 'spiritual awakening.' Some catalyst, often but not necessarily a confrontation with death, catapults us into a higher frequency state. Another way this can happen is in true Love with another – when we get to see the deep, authentic beauty of another human being and when the other holds up the mirror to show us the deep, authentic beauty of ourselves. We also receive little reminders every single day when we receive glimpses of Spirit in the kindness of a stranger, in the smile of a child, in the friskiness of a kitten, in the cherry blossoms against the blue sky, in the high of a moment performing on stage or at the finish line of a race...and we're abruptly catapulted into a higher, transcendental energy state. Thereafter it's up to us to hold and embody this higher energetic state, to sing the high melody!

While the practices described in the previous section can help us elevate our energy frequency closer to Love, holding it there can be challenging. A powerful way to always sing the melody of Love is to embody the principles of Wholeness, Abundance, Gratitude, and Resonance. I've written about these principles at length in my book *Thrive!*, and I'll cover them here again briefly.

Wholeness is the awareness of being perfect and complete as-is. Nobody is incomplete or lost, even if he or she has temporarily forgotten their completeness, or lost their way. When we can see both ourselves and others in this way, we remain in the frequency of Love. Abundance is the quality of both oneself and the Universe to contain limitless resources – there is no dearth of Love energy! When we remember this, physical resources also become abundant. Gratitude is the natural outcome of knowing Wholeness and Abundance, and being in a constant state of thanksgiving is a surefire way to stay in the energetic vibration of Love. (In fact, if you want to simplify things and do only *one* thing, do this –practice constant gratitude. It is powerful beyond measure!) Finally, when you are in constant touch with Wholeness, Abundance and Gratitude, you are automatically in Resonance with Spirit, always in the high vibration of Love, always a powerful, loving co-creator with Spirit.

Finally, one of the best ways to sing the melody of Love, to hold its high vibration, is to remember and embody – at every moment without exception – your true nature as a (creative) soul rather than a (reactive) body, mind or personality. As French philosopher Pierre Telhard de Chardin wrote in *The Phenomenon of Man*,

"We are not human beings having a spiritual experience, we are spiritual beings having a human experience."

As soon as we forget this and become identified with our physical, mental and emotional existence, forgetting that those are merely experiences of the soul in this material world, we collapse into the lower vibration. This is because physicality is the densest form of energy. Emotional and mental components of our existence are slightly higher in vibration, and the highest vibration is at the level of spirit, of our inner light.

Along with knowing your true nature as a soul created in Love, also remember the *qualities* of the soul. The original qualities of the soul, emanating from our true nature of Love, are Peace, Purity, Joy, Insight, Truth, and Power. The soul is always peaceful, no matter what storm is being faced by the body or personality it inhabits. The soul is pure and untarnished regardless of the blemishes and scars of the body and personality it wears. In this ever peaceful and pure state, the soul is always joyful. From this loving, peaceful, pure and joyful state, the soul has its inherent insight, for Spirit speaks to it directly, guiding it always to the truth of every moment. And from here, the soul has the power to create. Always remember your soulful nature, and you'll be able to create – everything from nothing.

REFLECTIONS

1   Imagine yourself as a musical instrument producing pleasant sound waves! Experiment with going about your day being that instrument, creating melody, harmony and positive resonance with those around you.

2   Close your eyes, breathe, and imagine yourself as the whole and complete Universe, at the center of which lies all abundance and all possibility. Notice the shift in your energy.

3   Connect with the possibility that you are a light-being, with your body being the vessel that holds this light. See this light in your mind's eye every day. Notice its color and intensity. Also notice the subtle sensations in your body when you do this.

PART II

EXERCISING YOUR CREATIVITY

There are many wonderful books and resources with strategic frameworks and specific tactics, exercises and practices for exercising creativity.[13] I find that no matter what the specific tips offered are, they can be broadly organized into two kinds of creative action, corresponding with two spiritual aspects of our existence, and of Love in action – be-ing and do-ing.

The be-ing stream of creative practices consists of the act of *receiving*. It involves lovingly stepping back to observe, study, reflect, venture within and even empty oneself, so that one may receive creative insight. The do-ing stream of practices consists of the act of *generating*. It involves lovingly stepping out to act, move, make, and manifest through persistent, committed, external expression, so that one may generate through external action. Somewhere between these two, is the magical heart of creativity – the mysterious process of *transforming* what is received or generated, into new meaning.

The receiving action, to a large extent, exercises intuitive knowing and the exploration of limitless possibility, while the generative action, to a large extent, exercises rational execution and tangible, expressed manifestation. The receiving action zooms way back in 'focal length' and the generative action zooms closely in with a macro lens to every detail.[14] Transformation into meaning requires a balance of both, and who knows exactly how?

For purposes of this discussion, let's explore the creative cycle in two aspects – a receiving-transforming action, corresponding to be-ing, and a generating-transforming

---

[13] At the end of this book, along with references, I've provided a list of my favorite books on practicing creativity.

[14] Read Twyla Tharp's beautiful explanation of this in terms of *zoe* and *bios*, in *The Creative Habit*, pages 42-44.

action, corresponding to do-ing. Those whose innate wiring leans toward the receiving-transforming action of creativity might celebrate the idea of the mad creative genius visited by the Muse, while those who lean toward the transforming-generating view of creativity might emphasize the 1%-inspiration-and-99%-perspiration view. But, getting carried away in the fallacy of duality, in the black-and-white division of the integrated creative force, risks oversimplification and error in true understanding.

The main insight I'd like to offer through this exploration is that in the most fully and powerfully expressed creative person, be-ing and do-ing become balanced, complementary and integrated. Be-ing is as *active* as do-ing; it is a concerted practice of creative stillness undertaken in pure awareness, a state of Love. And do-ing is another expression of Love; it is conscious, directed, and disciplined external action rather than the incessant busywork often associated with today's fast-paced world. So, embodying one's full creativity involves constantly practicing both the receiving-transforming and the generating-transforming abilities within oneself, and eventually finding balance and seamless integration between them, so they can be unified in one beautiful dance.

I find that a rich way to understand these complementary aspects of the practice of creativity is to explore them in terms of Yin and Yang – the creative feminine and the creative masculine forces at play within each of us. After all, these two forces in balance and complementarity make for Oneness and Love![15] Wikipedia explains the ancient Chinese and Asian philosophy of Yin Yang as such:

---

[15] Please note that this exploration is not about gender or physical sex, but may incidentally shed light for you on the social construct of gender, which has lost sight of the masculine-feminine in each of us no matter what physical sex we're expressed in, or gender we identify with.

"Yin Yang are not opposing forces (dualities), but complementary opposites, unseen (hidden, feminine) and seen (manifest, masculine), that interact within a greater whole, as part of a dynamic system."

In other words, Yin, the feminine principle, provides the landscape of limitless possibility, while Yang, the masculine principle, provides the impetus via conscious intention. Spiritually speaking, when Yin and Yang interact in Love, intention fuses with possibility to manifest a particular instance of creation. Just as both the feminine and masculine energies are required for procreation, so are they for creation!

The Yin, or the creative feminine, is the be-ing force, and acts by stepping back and venturing within into the void, to be primarily in receiving mode. It also transforms what it receives, such as within the womb. Its natural forte is intuitive knowing. The Yang, or the creative masculine, is the do-ing force, and acts by stepping out for external action, to do in generative mode. It transforms even as it generates. Its natural forte is manifest expression.

I find that a meta-level understanding of our inner creative resources in terms of Yin and Yang is very useful because once you understand yourself in these terms, you can easily develop your own strategies, tactics, exercises and practices corresponding to each aspect working within you. You can discover if you lean more heavily toward one aspect over another, and seek to balance and integrate the two aspects within yourself. The specific practices and exercises you develop will then be unique to you and your natural inclinations. And if you're borrowing them from other people writing about or teaching creativity, you'll still know where their recommendations fall within your Yin-Yang expression.

Once you locate both feminine and masculine principles of creativity within yourself and in your practices, you'll achieve a balance of Yin-Yang energy, ensuring the full use of your inner creative resources. You will find that both aspects are being equally developed and expressed. And with deeper practice you will be able to seamlessly integrate them, and bring them to bear simultaneously in your way of creating. Spiritually speaking, becoming whole within ourselves is essential to becoming One with Spirit, and thereby also becoming a conscious and powerful co-creator with Spirit.

The significance of Yin-Yang balance and integration as the way to fully exercise my creativity spontaneously opened up for me in recent years as I ventured deeper into extensive creative and spiritual work, holding the frequency of Love. It became clear that thriving as a creative, vibrant and spiritually alive being includes embodying both the feminine and masculine principles in balance and integration. It also became apparent that such balance is terribly important to bring to the mass consciousness, because in general, humanity (men and women alike), has veered excessively toward manifest, external action (Yang), and has forgotten to access the power of the unseen, of limitless possibility (Yin). Things that were commonplace in tribal cultures such as the ancient understanding of Mother Earth, being viscerally in touch with Nature's cycles and cosmic forces, harnessing the power of the lunar cycle, and so on, have withered. With the advent of modern science, we live in a culture that places a much higher value on rational thinking and scientific rigor (Yang) than the deep reserves of intuitive wisdom and innate connection with Nature we come equipped with (Yin).

Ironically, even movements of social reform such as feminism, which sought to 'fight' the dominance of masculine energy, have merely embodied more Yang energy! They have mirrored and strengthened its external-action orientation and sheer muscle and will, neglecting to exercise the true power of Yin energy, which is located in the void, the stillness, the unseen. As such, the feminist movement's underpinnings are essentially *more* masculine, Yang energy being wielded in action. Of course you cannot fight Yang with Yang; you must neutralize and balance it with Yin! This is why this movement has had limited success in bringing about true balance, integration and harmony.

As a woman, it was ironic that finding an appropriate inner balance between the Yin and Yang forces within myself, actually began with reconnecting with my Yin – owning and celebrating the feminine within me! I discovered that my upbringing and academic training had overdeveloped my Yang aspect and entirely neglected my Yin aspect. I had leaned far, far out to mental analytics and externally manifest action – that is, into my Yang – and had neglected to access, cultivate, or trust my still, unseen, intuitive wisdom, of which I naturally had a deep resource, including the gift of uncanny, extra-sensory perception. Also, in finding my Yin-Yang balance, I was called to transcend both the identity of the oppressed, victimized woman of time-immemorial, as well as the relatively recent identity of the progressive, equal-to-man feminist, valiantly fighting for fair rights and status.

Having found a balance, I was able to practice the Yang aspect of my creativity with much greater awareness and intention, guided and supported by the infinite wisdom of the Yin aspect. Once I had practiced being in my Yin aspect long enough, I was also able to move between Yin and Yang with fluidity, calibrating and fine-tuning my understanding of timing and context-appropriateness of one aspect over the other. Eventually, I was able to bring them to bear simultaneously and complementarily, in complete integration. Like the expert martial artist, I began to see when to exert external action, and when to receive the force exerted upon me to make it *my* internal power!

Leveraging the Yin creative principle involves cultivating the fertile soil of creation on an ongoing basis. The loving expression of the Yin principle requires one to learn creative stillness, the art of recognizing and receiving the Muse, and then, channeling it through oneself to birth an act of creation. In your feminine aspect, you must act as a magnetic stillness, innately knowing visionary, a spark of inspiration, a catalyst for change, the sensor of subtlety, and the medium of flow, order and life force for humankind's highest potential.[16]

Leveraging the Yang principle involves executing through creative action, that which has been revealed through creative stillness. For the loving expression of your masculine aspect, you must act as the passionate seeker, the discoverer, the leader by example, and the creator of something greater than yourself, for the manifest expression of humankind's highest potential.[17]

So, practicing creativity in the Yin aspect is like cultivating the soil, while practicing creativity in the Yang aspect is like planting the seed. Both go hand in hand for the seed to sprout into a seedling, and then grow into a tree that bears fruit!

It is this special ability to discern the difference between the Yin and Yang aspects of creativity, to recognize when to lovingly invoke which, and find the delicate dance between them at all times, that I attempt to convey in the following chapters. For each Yin practice in Chapter Three, there is a corresponding and complementary Yang practice in

---

[16] Inspired by spiritual teacher and intuitive healer Jenna Forrest's online audio teachings on finding the creative feminine and masculine within. See: http://profoundhealingforsensitives.com/

[17] Same as previous note.

Chapter Four. The practices I write about are relatively generic. Once you understand the idea behind each of these, you'll find that you're easily able to interpret other writers' and teachers' practices as Yin or Yang actions, as well as develop your own. The framework I offer here is a start, based on my personal experience and insights thus far.

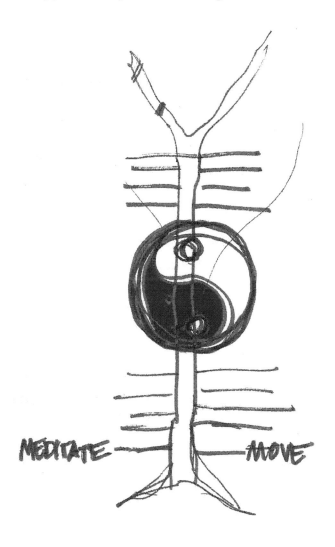

3

INNER ACTION

THE CREATIVE YIN

"Never mistake motion for action."
– Ernest Hemingway

"Think like a man of action; act like a man of thought."
– Henri Bergson

"The intuitive mind tells the thinking mind where to go next."
– Jonas Salk

1
MEDITATE
... MOVE [YANG]

The one-word action that best represents the feminine or Yin principle of creativity is: Meditate!

Generally speaking, meditation is the practice of becoming a neutral observer to whatever arises when we step back and hold an intentional stillness. Neutrality is the key qualifier;[18] it is an easily overlooked yet tremendously powerful quality of Love. It creates the whitespace – the blank canvas – for all possibility to emerge. It allows someone or something to be what it must naturally and organically be. It channels pure awareness, and therefore, limitless creativity.

In the recent book *Mastermind: How To Think Like Sherlock Holmes*, science writer Maria Konnikova explores the importance of distance, mindfulness and Observation with a capital 'O' in creativity, by examining the habits of Sir Arthur Conan Doyle's much loved detective. When we work in our regular consciousness, the brain emits beta waves, but in a meditative state, the brain emits alpha waves and delta waves, which access our higher consciousness. Konnikova writes:

"In recent years studies have shown that meditation-like thought...for as little as fifteen minutes a day, can shift frontal brain activity toward a pattern that has been associated with more positive and more approach-oriented

---

[18] In Vipassana meditation, the central idea is to observe bodily sensations with complete neutrality – neither craving, nor aversion. The arising experiential realization is that everything in material reality is *anicca* (impermanent) and *anatta* (impersonal).

emotional states, and that looking at scenes of nature, for even a short while, can help us become more insightful, more creative, and more productive."

Unconscious processing is required for ideas to align, Konnikova says; therefore, distance is a huge facilitator of imaginative thinking. In my personal experience, thanks to my frequent and often spontaneous meditative states, 'strokes of genius' and insight 'download' into my consciousness as if from nowhere and in no-time, things that don't come to me from effortful doing, and certainly not from busywork. So, to me, being a creative person and not having some kind of meditative practice is simply untenable, because meditation is fundamental to be-ing and receiving. The Muse can only get through to those who truly listen, and meditation is the ultimate state of neutral, evaluation-free, active listening.

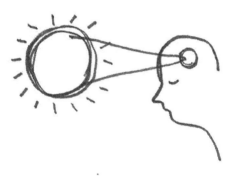

Meditation connects us with our infinite being, with the limitless landscape of possibility, and with Spirit. Meditation expands and strengthens awareness, imagination, observation, and insight like nothing else does. Without listening for all the incredible clues, patterns, whispers, messages, insights...that are lurking within our own higher consciousness and within the greater order and intelligence of the Universe, there can be no quantum jumps, no new ideas and connections, and no new ways of looking at things. So, meditation is indispensable to creativity, for receiving, and for transforming what is received.

What form of meditation you choose, and how formal a practice it is, is really up to your natural inclinations and preferences. There is no right or wrong way other than the intention, commitment and dedication to your practice. It can be anything as simple as gazing out to the sea or out to a green landscape, to observing your breath, to using a chant to focus the mind, to holding a monotone melody. I personally prefer forms that use one's body and breath and no other external aids, as taught in the ancient tradition of Vipassana. It's important to know the difference between meditation and contemplation; the latter involves reflecting and focusing on a particular idea or thought in stillness, while the former is a way of fully emptying oneself into neutrality and thereby gaining access to a higher, more universal intelligence, which allows for an expanded awareness of all possibility.

Every practice I enlist hereafter in this chapter, is some specific variant of this very important action of be-ing that cultivates our creativity in richly significant ways.

2
EMPTY YOURSELF FOR STILLNESS...

...JUST DO IT, JUST TO DO IT [YANG]

In the intense period after releasing my second book *Thrive!*, I found my creativity being expressed as a meditation, involving patiently and lovingly holding a space of intense stillness, and seeing what is revealed as the next thing. But wait, being creative is about *producing* something, right? So how can creativity be expressed as stillness?

Consider how, to nurture the fertility of their land, farmers cycle crops and then allow for a season or two of no crops. Mother Earth, Nature's best example of a prolific and fertile womb of creation, also needs a break – a break for stillness and replenishment, a break to pause and take stock of what she's inclined to grow and produce next. Creative stillness, therefore, is the loving cultivation of intuition, receptivity, and fertility. Without creative stillness, the Muse wouldn't be heard, no idea would be recognized or envisioned, and there would be no fertile womb to seed and nurture it in, either. So, as a creative person, one must periodically and intentionally empty oneself, and step into creative stillness.

Most of the intensely creative people I've seen grow through the Creativity Workshops I coach, have faced what they initially think are empty or unproductive periods in their creative cycles. It's easy to feel stuck, assuming that if you're not engaged in external creative action, you're being uncreative. But, when you begin to honor this phase as an active, creative stillness, all sorts of new connections and insights open up.

Therefore, a period of be-ing, of intentional stillness and replenishment, is not only necessary for creativity, but it is an integral and *active* part of being creative. Creative stillness is not to be mistaken either as passive or as the benign pause between bursts of 'real' creativity, but as an intentional, equal and complementary half to external creative action. It is part and parcel of the full cycle of creativity.

Cultivating creative stillness has three significant aspects:

AWARENESS

Awareness allows us to watch ourselves. Simply being able to witness and experience ourselves and our surroundings with an expanded awareness provides larger access to Spirit, and channels much reception and transformation. In the next essay, I'll discuss awareness in fuller detail.

PRESENCE

The act of witnessing in awareness automatically makes us present to the Now. Presence immediately connects us with Spirit and cultivates the fertile soil of creativity. Even with no external action, Presence alone transforms what is received, into meaningful insight.

INTENTION

In awareness and presence, one can hold conscious intention, which prepares us fully for the channeling of the Muse into external creative action. Intention develops our ability to transform what is received, into generative content. Intention is the genesis of all creation – every creation will always bear the energetic imprint of its intention.

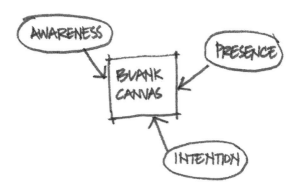

Together, awareness, presence and intention ensure that we see the unusual in the mundane, that we connect the dots in new and meaningful ways, and that we know intuitively which opportunity presents the most potential – all hallmarks of creative genius!

CREATIVE EXPERIMENT

Through the Creativity Workshops, Sheeba Marie Jacob created and launched her first ever music CD, *Sing it From Your Soul*. Then she found that in the period after releasing her CD, external creative action began to feel more like busywork rather than intentional and purposeful, like it had been when she was working on the production. As soon as she recognized this, she stopped acting outwardly and moved into inner stillness. It took her several months of watchful, intentional stillness to reconnect with the landscape of possibility, and then authentic creative action began to come forth once again. At the time of this writing, Sheeba has embarked on a project of interviewing couples for their love stories, with a plan to transform these into lyrics for a new collection of songs!

3
EXPAND YOUR AWARENESS...
...AND DO IT DAILY [YANG]

Most limitations to our creativity come from a state of contraction in awareness related to fear. Such a state prevents us from seeing possibility. Moving into Love, therefore, involves opening ourselves and expanding our awareness. As we explored in the previous essay, expanding awareness is a significant aspect of practicing creative stillness, which cultivates the landscape and allows the creative seeds sown to have a life.

In *Spiritual Solutions*, Deepak Chopra proposes that there are three states of awareness: contracted awareness, expanded awareness, and pure awareness.[19] Each of these states corresponds to a level of energy vibration, a frequency of melody, if you will. Chopra says that in the state of contracted awareness we perceive problems. In the state of expanded awareness we are able to see solutions. In a state of pure awareness, however, there are no problems to begin with, only possibility and pure creativity!

As with everything else, the best way to gauge one's energy or frequency level is to check in with one's feelings. In contracted awareness, Chopra says, one feels separate from the Universe and Spirit and other beings. A sign of being in this state is a feeling of being stuck – when the more you struggle to get free of a problem the more you are trapped into it. In this state we often contract our bodies as well.

In expanded awareness one feels connected, while still being aware of one's individual, separate existence. A good sign that you are generally in this state is when the feeling of stuckness disappears, a process of solution-making begins to unfold, and unseen forces easily come to your aid. Think of all the moments in which "time stops still," and you are "in the zone." Or think of when you take a leap of faith into the unknown and suddenly there is no difference between you and your environment because all of it is one big mush. Or think of the moment in which you see into the deep, pure, soulful beauty of another and he is able to see into you too, and suddenly there is no separation between the two of you; all that exists does so within the Oneness of the

---

[19] See pages 4-10 of Chopra's book *Spiritual Solutions* for more in-depth explanations. Also watch: http://www.youtube.com/watch?v=E83QK8wwFsI

interaction. This is the moment of Love, the moment of expanded awareness, when virtually anything feels possible. While such moments of expanded awareness are fleetingly available to many of us, Chopra says that "...expanded awareness should be our normal state, not a moment of extraordinary difference. Making it normal is the whole point of the spiritual life," and I would add, of the creative life.

The ultimate level is pure, unmediated awareness. In pure awareness you become One with Spirit. It is a completely struggle-free state wherein desires are fulfilled spontaneously, and you are fully at home in the Universe. Enlightenment, Chopra says, is essentially the equivalent of being completely established in this state of pure awareness.

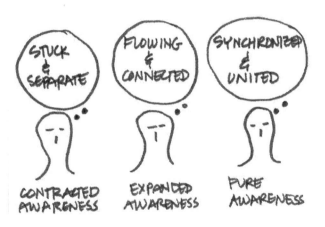

In my personal experience, expanding awareness seems to be a singularly Yin-based endeavor. Chopra proposes that awareness can be expanded by observing the thoughts and feelings generated by one's perceptions, assumptions, expectations, and beliefs.[20] If these make one feel contracted, with downward-spiral type of thinking, then one is in contracted awareness. If these make one feel confident and enthusiastic, and inspired to conjure up ideas and possibilities to make the most of a situation, one is in expanded awareness. In pure awareness, perceptions, assumptions, expectations and beliefs disappear, and there is nothing but silent witnessing, beyond subject-object split.[21] This is transcendence, and anything becomes possible, including pure, limitless creative potential. It is in this realm of uncertainty – the quantum field – that discrete, discontinuous leaps of creativity become possible. These are the leaps of faith and Love that we believe to be extraordinary exceptions in our typical experience. In an enlightened state, however, these make for a constant way of being.

CREATIVE EXPERIMENT

In the two years in which I've published my previous book *Thrive!* and written this one, my condominium complex was diagnosed with a significant water seepage problem in its building envelope. The homeowners' association undertook an extensive investigation, litigation and then construction process, during which the entire building was wrapped in tarp, noise, dust...you name it. This also placed significant financial burdens on homeowners like me, who now owed the association large sums of money for their share of the project. During this period, my design strategy consulting work was hardly consistent, and it would've been easy to cave in and return to a more secure job. But, at this time my work in writing and publishing, visual art, and music training and teaching, as well as facilitating Creativity Workshops,

---

[20] See pages 10-14 of Chopra's book *Spiritual Solutions* for more in-depth explanations. Also watch:
http://www.youtube.com/watch?v=wSNk9z4Ew60
[21] In Chapter One I discussed specific approaches and methods for recognizing and clearing feelings, and in Chapter Two, approaches to transmuting beliefs and expanding awareness and energy.

was in an all-time growth spurt. If I gave it up at that time, I would miss cashing out on the true riches of several years of preparation and cultivation.

I constantly experimented with my levels of awareness through daily, intense meditation and stillness. And something miraculous would often happen. Even as I sat in my living room enveloped by thick tarp and men hanging off my little deck, there would be moments in which the tarp and men would completely disappear from my view, and I'd be able to 'see' beyond. I would literally see my view of First Avenue, Mt. Rainier, and the Puget Sound restored. The phrase, "This is not happening at all!" would keep flashing in my mind's eye. "This is a play with a stage set, and these are characters playing temporary roles, hanging off your deck." Through this entire time, I managed to complete a consulting project, teach and perform music on stage, paint and exhibit my art and even have it adopted, write this book, and also undertake a significant international trip. All the help I needed with places to stay, people to host my petrified feline friends, and a loan to cover the extra cost, materialized on their own in just the right times.

In those moments of immense clarity when everything in my near sight disappeared and my long view was restored, I knew I was connected with pure awareness, the level at which there are no problems to begin with. This is hardly denial, because I could well see and hear the tremendously invasive activity. Rather, it is a *seeing beyond* to know that there is nothing 'wrong' at all to begin with, that at the level of soul, this 'reality' is actually temporary illusion, like a scrape on my body that will quickly and naturally heal and disappear.

4
RECOGNIZE SYNCHRONICITY...
...CONNECT THE DOTS [YANG]

From continuous practice, I've discovered that an immediate corollary to holding creative stillness and expanding awareness is the increased appearance of meaningful coincidences, serendipity, and miraculous alignments in space and time, what in religious terms has been understood as moments of Grace. Synchronicity is a term that encompasses the range of such experiences, and was originally coined by one of my most revered creative spiritualists, parapsychologist Carl Gustav Jung.[22]

When you are in pure awareness, suddenly, it is almost as if everything, both in the external world and in your internal intuitive thoughts, is speaking directly to you, and is benevolently said or written or visualized *exactly* for your situation, for your healing, for your learning and listening, and for your creative action. Signs lovingly show up everywhere, as if to inform you, guide you, and lead you, always just in time. And outcomes manifest with remarkable speed and ease, with uncanny, precise timing and little to no struggle on your part. This is the state of being in synchronicity.

Jung posited that synchronistic events reveal an underlying pattern, a conceptual framework that encompasses but is larger than any of the systems that display the synchronicity. This suggestion of a larger framework is

---

[22] Per Wikipedia at the time of this writing, "Synchronicity is the experience of two or more events that are apparently causally unrelated or unlikely to occur together by chance, yet are experienced as occurring together in a meaningful manner. The concept of synchronicity was first described in this terminology by Carl Gustav Jung, a Swiss psychologist, in the 1920s."

essential to satisfy his definition of synchronicity, and in my experience, this is the larger Spirit and Love I have so palpably felt connected with when I am being and creating in expanded awareness.

Recently, my sister Sharmishtha, a professor of Geo-Biology in The University of Göttingen at the time of this writing, (synchronously!) pointed me to the extensive work of Joseph Jaworski. Not only has he written books such as *Synchronicity* and *Source*, but he has also established a successful global leadership forum based on getting answers from time in nature, meditation, and Qi Gong.[23]

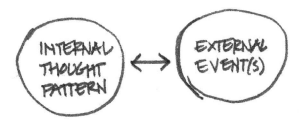

In my direct experience I find that being in synchronicity means that you have suddenly become aligned with the natural flow of the Universe; you've connected with its ever-giving, limitless wellspring of Love. You've tuned your personal melody into resonance and harmony with Divine Music. Like the many radio waves available in the air, messages are constantly available for you; it is a matter of tuning in to find the frequency match. When you do so, you're dancing in tandem with Spirit itself. In the state of synchronicity, you are bound to "hear the music" and "see the light" differently. This is a state of intense inspiration and creativity, because the Muse is speaking directly to you! And

---

[23] Joseph Jaworski's now international company has grown substantially and eventually split into parts, one of which is Reos Partners, a social innovation consultancy. See: http://reospartners.com

you are in the mode of quiet, active, intentional, loving listening, allowing the higher guidance to come forth, seed your womb, and reveal a path for creative action.

In her famous TED talk on 'genius,'[24] Elizabeth Gilbert describes how the Romans believed genius to be a magical, divine entity who literally lived in the walls of a creative person's studio, and invisibly assisted the artist with his work. This notion of a visiting genius is the Muse I am referring to, and consistent with the phenomenon of synchronicity, in which we tune in to our very own personal radio channel – the creative guidance of Spirit uniquely available to each of us.

While one might slip into synchronicity spontaneously or as an organic outcome of intensely practicing creative stillness and awareness, the greater challenge lies in recognizing the guidance within the messages coming your way. By themselves, the messages may even appear meaningless if your ability to transform them into something meaningful for you isn't well developed. This includes discerning the difference between what is meant for your silent knowing and holding, and what is meant for either immediate, or long-range external action.[25]

I find that sharpening my abilities for observation and active listening through meditation, walking outdoors, doing yoga and other such contemplative physical movement, helps me know the intention of various messages. Faith that I will be

---

[24] Watch: http://www.ted.com/talks/elizabeth_gilbert_on_genius.html

[25] Recently I was gifted this insight regarding the nuanced but significant difference between signs and synchronicity. Signs are pointers and clues to immediate creative action in the Now, not necessarily revealing any higher order pattern or meaning for your life, or future. They are meant to be faithfully followed without attachment to outcome. Synchronicities are evidence of a higher order pattern emerging, and manifesting as certain outcomes. Synchronicities guide us toward receiving this pattern into our lives, and also toward aligning our creative actions, if any are required at all, with the greater order.

shown the best way allows me to either continue holding stillness or take external action with confidence, in accordance with the messages I've received. Either way, being in synchronicity means that one is in a space of intense creativity, because the Universe's intention for loving, creative action is being communicated directly to and through you!

CREATIVE EXPERIMENT

For Rashmi Thirtha Jyoti, the six weeks of Creativity Workshops successfully launched *Shringaara*, a jewelry line incorporating the healing power of gemstones. A few months later, she experienced a period of complete stagnation. The motivation to create new jewelry pieces simply wouldn't flow. Sleep was elusive; she was restless and frustrated. She even experienced intense periods of ill health and grief. Rashmi went into hibernation, a period of stillness and being fully present with patience and Love, which expanded her awareness. After nine months, suddenly, creations and messages started flowing through. The 'downloads' came to her at great speed, and she began writing, sketching, and painting. She was channeling beautiful, colorful *mandalas* in great detail, in her meditation hours. She also felt directed to study sacred geometry, and so, began research on Sacred Geometry and Mandalas. Then came the synchronicity! The Women of Wisdom Conference happened in Seattle, and Rashmi signed up without a thought. The conference had workshops on healing, creativity and mandalas, everything exactly matching her inner guidance! At the time of this writing, Rashmi's jewelry line is being re-born with a new name and logo tying her newest insights together. In parallel, she has also launched a space for women called 'Women's Sacred Sanctuary,' to tap into and share stories of intuitive insight and healing. This is a monthly event that in just two months has already become a well-attended one.

5
INVITE, ENROLL AND PREPARE TO RECEIVE...
...CONTRIBUTE TO A POSITIVE SUM GAME [YANG]

If synchronicity is the state of listening for and recognizing the Universe's intention for creative action, then the next thing to do is to prepare yourself to become the loving womb, the channel, for the actual seeding and gestation of such intention. To do so, you must be in a constant state of preparation and open invitation. You must create a healthy space within yourself to receive. You must gently and actively nurture the heart-womb for ideas and inspirations to take root.

In the TED talk on genius by Elizabeth Gilbert that I referenced earlier, she describes her conversation with poet Ruth Stone. Stone told Gilbert that she would often find herself visited unexpectedly by a poem while working in the open fields of rural Virginia, and be forced to go running home, chased by the poem, rushing to find pen and paper before it found another poet! And sometimes, Stone told Gilbert, she had to catch a poem by its tail as it whooshed past her. On these occasions, it came to her backwards! What Stone is really describing is the incredible level of awareness and preparation it takes to be available to the Muse at all times. In *The Law of Divine Compensation*, Marianne Williamson writes,

"Spirit can only channel through a prepared vessel."

In the language of procreation, this preparation is the feminine process of developing your prenatal health, readying the womb for receiving sperm and forming a healthy fetus.

YOU ARE MICHELANGELO...AND YOU ARE DAVID!

Just like you take vitamins, eat, rest and exercise well, keep positive and healthy company, consume the right information-diet, connect with family, and so on, preparing to receive the Muse is a similarly invested endeavor of loving self-care!

For instance, very few lists on how to enhance your creativity contain the recommendation to get lots of sleep. In fact, the stereotype of the creative genius is one who barely needs three hours of sleep and is madly making away at all odd hours. But sleep is a tremendously significant aspect of creating a healthy, receptive womb for creativity! It is actually an incredibly creative time because it brings our vast subconscious into play. Dream states are prolifically creative states, and our spirits both send and receive all sorts of messages during this time. Over time I've developed a strong intuitive sense that my spirit even travels in other dimensions during my sleep, something possible only when our conscious minds with their limited belief systems are put to rest, literally and otherwise! Therefore, healthy sleep is a significant requirement for creating an inviting, receptive space that is capable of channeling and hosting the Muse.

Walking is a surprisingly simple, unexpected and understated external activity that powerfully catalyzes a healthy womb for receiving the Muse. As Nipun Mehta said in his unusual and moving convocation speech titled *Paths are Made by Walking*,[26] and delivered to University of Pennsylvania graduates in 2012, walking is the pace at which humans were designed to experience the physical world. It is the pace at which we witness, connect with ourselves, and recognize signs and messages for action. Mairah Kalhman, prolific author and illustrator, insists that walking is one of the most significant activities that boosts creativity.

---

[26] Read the full transcript of Nipun Mehta's speech at:
http://www.dailygood.org/view.php?sid=236

Walking outside along the water (since I have the fortune of living in heavenly Seattle) is my favorite form of movement in service of my creativity. Not only do I get physical exercise and fresh air, something always clicks in my mind-body-spirit complex in inexplicable ways, whenever I'm walking outside. Inevitably, whatever I just "walked away from" gains new and exponential momentum when I return. I recall a recent experience on a waterfront walk: A melody I was working on, an idea for a poster design, and the stanza of a poem all visited me simultaneously! I had no pen or paper on me (something I'm learning quickly is an absolute must on my walks), so I had to draw out the concept for the poster in the sand in order to make a photographic imprint of it in my memory, keep humming the melody, and then run back home in a hurry like Ruth Stone, to catch the poem by its tail![27] The day had been apparently unproductive until that time in the waning Seattle winter afternoon, and suddenly, the evening hours gave birth to three different things!

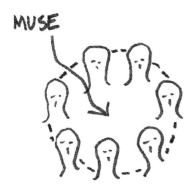

MUSE

Another aspect of creating a space of receiving is lovingly building creative communities by enrolling other kindred creative spirits as well as audiences for one's work,

---

[27] Now that I think of it, that poem, titled *For Every Kind of Mother*, did get written backwards, last stanza first!

which generates a synergistic pool of collective creative resources and energy. Lisa Gansky writes in *The Mesh* that the cutting-edge of entrepreneurial ventures is also located in this idea of synergistic networks with pooling of resources, both between businesses and between businesses and their audiences or patrons.[28]

Much like a positive and supportive friendship- or family-network nurtures a healthy prenatal space, so does periodically connecting with other creative people and their endeavors, nurture one's own creative womb with the right nutrients. One of the biggest assets of the Creativity Workshops, more than my coaching itself, is the collective creative energy generated in the room for a sustained period of time, which deeply feeds and nurtures the inner creative spaces of all participants, including me. Connecting in this way also creates investment – each participant becomes invested in the creative success of the other, as well as of the group as a whole. This summons Spirit's powers in a big way, because of the synergy already forming through the individual spirits communing. Such communion unleashes an enormous, exponential power, which aids in manifesting the collective vision for a creative, thriving human existence on this planet.

One's audience also forms a body of powerful co-creators. I've discovered that the real reason to publish or ship (as marketing guru and bestselling author Seth Godin calls it) a creative product is less about changing the world (and certainly not about accolades or remuneration or fame), but more about lovingly serving and growing the creative act itself. In the beautiful book *Finding the Sweet Spot*, Dave Pollard writes about pathfinders – people who show up as you navigate your soul path, to point the way, to tell you about what the Universe needs; in short, to co-create with you. The

---

[28] Examples of businesses built on the mesh model are Netflix and Zipcar.

audience is actually a part of this body of pathfinders that makes it all happen for the creator.

In the tremendously rich and generous blog and newsletter *Brain Pickings,* curator-editor Maria Popova writes about Marcel Duchamp's reading of his paper *The Creative Act.*[29] In this essay, Duchamp speaks of the artist's "mediumistic role," and how "the spectator brings the work in contact with the external world by deciphering and interpreting its inner qualifications and this adds his contribution to the creative act." So, no creative product or endeavor is complete without its interaction with an audience, no matter how small this interaction, or what it looks like.

Graduates of the Creativity Workshops I facilitate always present their work in a project showcase. And personally, every piece of writing or art I make must be published or shown, the music I learn must be performed or otherwise shared through teaching, and most of all, all insights I gain on leading a creative life must be articulated and shared in some form or another. And this must happen all the time, throughout my life!

CREATIVE EXPERIMENT

Creativity Workshop participant Sheeba Marie Jacob finds that while working on creative projects, enrolling others immediately works wonders. For example, when she was looking to find a recording studio to produce her CD, her brother connected her to a friend who records music. He in turn offered the services of his wife, a graphic designer, to design the CD cover. When Sheeba was looking for a space to host her CD release party, her friend Tasha immediately

---

[29] See: http://www.brainpickings.org/index.php/2012/08/23/the-creative-act-marcel-duchamp-1957/

mentioned a cafe where another music show was scheduled, and the café owner readily agreed to also host Sheeba's release party as well. When she was looking for a photographer, friend and co-creative Sudha said she would be happy to take photos at the event. There was no struggle in finding all required resources; Sheeba just had to consider the big picture, enroll her community for support, and let the rest flow.

6

CHANNEL THE MUSE THROUGH...

...SCULPT AWAY THE DEBRIS [YANG]

Following the creation of a healthy womb is the actual act of conception! This allowing of an idea to seed and then nurturing it to full form is an exquisitely and deeply enjoyable feminine action. Like bringing an offspring into being, there are significant milestones in making a creative offering to the world, each with its own challenges, pains and joys – conception, gestation and delivery!

I've discovered that the most challenging aspect of creating in the highest plane is discerning the difference between self-conscious doing and allowing the Muse to channel through in a way that one becomes purely a medium of higher expression. In pure creativity, one must surrender one's ego personality and fixed idea of what the outcome should be, to the higher creative process occurring *through* oneself, rather than *by* one. This doesn't mean that one's individuality and singularity are irrelevant, for the creation will always bear the imprint of its mother. Rather, this is about knowing that one's higher self will know exactly what to do when one's willy-nilly whims and preferences are moved out of the way. I describe this awareness further in the following essay, *Distinguish free will from flow*, as well as in the corresponding Yang principle in the following chapter, *Sculpt Away the Debris*.

Once a creative idea has seeded, it must be appropriately gestated, and then birthed at the right time. The gestation period is about showing up to do the work with discipline and commitment, which is the job of the Yang principle. And then, the responsibility of the Yin principle is to discern when a creative product is actually finished and ready to emerge into the world. This can be a big ego trap, tricky to recognize. It is so easy to get caught up in perfectionism, making the object of one's creation that one bit better, crossing those last ts, adding that last brush stroke, sanding down that last bit of wood, and so on. Here's what to remember: Something isn't finished because it is perfect for the world. Something is finished when it exhibits signs of being done living inside you, and ready to have an independent life, ready to *interact* with the world and become its own thing through this interaction. The ability to recognize and follow these signs is the difference between (the potential narcissism of) perfectionism, and true creativity. Louis Kahn, one of my heroes in the world of architecture, has said: [30]

"...a building has to start in the unmeasurable aura and go through the measurable to be accomplished. It is the only way you can build. The only way you can get it into being is through the measurable. You must follow the laws, but in the end, when the building becomes part of the living, it evokes unmeasurable qualities. The design involving

---

[30] Louis I. Kahn, quoted in Green, "Louis I. Kahn, Architect," 3.

quantities of brick, method of construction, engineering is ended and the spirit of its existence takes over."

Another artist of historic fame, Wassily Kandinsky, has said the same thing but with direct reference to the mystical ways of Spirit:

"The true work of art is born from the 'artist': a mysterious, enigmatic, and mystical creation. It detaches itself from him, it acquires an autonomous life, becomes a personality, an independent subject, animated with a spiritual breath, the living subject of a real existence of being."

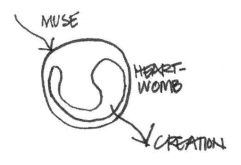

Creativity, then, is not about being right! It is about lovingly allowing what has channeled through you from Spirit, to take tangible form and live a life of its own. It is about trusting that if it was conceived in Love, it will be right even if imperfect. So, just like there is such a thing as too soon for a new life to emerge from its mother's womb, there is also such a thing as too late. Even if it comes out kicking and screaming in a bloody mess, come out it must! Imagine trying to keep your baby inside you *just a tad longer* after your water has broken, because you think you can make it that much stronger or that much cleverer, or that much more beautiful. That's what perfectionism is like! Instead, the act of detached letting go, so that the creative product can take on a life of its own, is an act of true Love.

So, what are the signs? How do I know my water has broken? I wish I could articulate it all as a rational, neatly packaged formula, but I cannot. It is different for every creative person, and for each object of her creation. This much I do know, though. There are distinct, intuitive and visceral feelings that you'll recognize if you've developed your Yin side well. An innate knowing that keeping something inside now has diminishing returns and no sustained purpose. A readiness to let go, to release. A curiosity and joy to stand back and witness the creation interact with the world. Also, a strange sense of already being *beyond* the object of creation, looking back at it with a healthy detachment. And finally, a joyful eagerness for continuing evolution through yet another iteration of creativity!

Leonardo Da Vinci, my personal creative hero, is known to have said, "Art is never finished, only abandoned." I'd rephrase Da Vinci's proclamation thus: "Art is never finished, only released."

7
DISTINGUISH FREE WILL FROM FLOW...
...MAKE DISCONTINUOUS, QUANTUM LEAPS [YANG]

Whether in stillness, or in conceiving an idea, or in allowing it to channel through into a product and then interact with audiences to have a life of its own, one of the key aspects of the creative feminine principle, is the ability to discern the difference between free will and flow. While the masculine principle's job is to put free will into external action, the feminine principle must intuitively connect with the higher Universal flow, so that one's free will action can be aligned in synchronicity with this greater order. I find this to be a big challenge for most, and a pretty significant discernment to develop in order to manifest the right creative outcomes with ease, and in harmony with the world.

We all have free will, and most of us know and recognize it well. It is an important aspect of our creative existence; we use it all the time to make conscious choice and generate action, to execute and follow through to manifest outcomes in certain directions over others, and so on.

We also have the Universe's higher order flow with specific implications for oneself. Some might call this destiny; I choose the term flow over destiny because the latter has come to mean in the minds of many, a fixed script pre-written by some higher entity, entirely without one's control. Instead, I sense that flow is one's own choice – a higher, soul-level choice – which is made in terms of creative life purpose, but is often forgotten in our limited, material-reality consciousness. It is the soul's blueprint, its DNA, waiting to *emerge through us*, as spiritual teacher Derek Rydall would put it, something we're here to re-member, and then embody. I sense that flow is also a constantly re-creating contract with the Universe – an individual soul purpose in dynamic interaction with the collective needs of the Universe in any given moment. So, flow is a live, dynamic thing, being created as we create!

The difference between free will and flow, then, is that free will exists at the material level of personality and ego, and can be exercised independent of soul purpose. Depending on one's level of awareness, free will can be used to aid, be apathetic to or ignorant of, or even to unconsciously resist or sabotage one's soul purpose! Most of the time, free will is slave to one's little self, operating in the area of survival – of one's ego, wants, needs and fears – even when one thinks it is being used to create 'positive' outcomes for the world! One's flow, however, is always in the direction of one's higher, soul purpose. And therefore, it is also naturally aligned with greater good, for both oneself and for the Universe. When we manifest depression, listlessness, disease or misfortune in life, it is usually our bodies' and minds' way of telling us that somewhere down the road, our free will has strayed way off the path charted by our flow, our soul purpose!

Thriving in creative power comes with recognizing the nature, direction and momentum of flow, and then humbly and gratefully aligning free will with that direction and momentum. This leads to a powerful synergy and exponential increase in one's ability to create the highest and best outcomes.

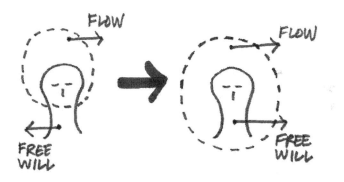

You know you are successful in discerning flow and aligning free will with it when events and outcomes manifest with ease and immediacy, without much struggle on your part. Sure, you do the hard work, but all effort is made in the area of your purpose and creative interest, not in tactics or maneuvers to manage and coax things into happening a particular way that you've deemed right. Synchronicity occurs – there is a greatly increased incidence of serendipity, coincidence and organically unfolding events. Other people step up to make things happen in tandem, in the direction of your flow. Whatever occurs feels like "just the right thing" and "in just the right time," even if it takes you by surprise and you feel momentarily unprepared to meet the challenge, or receive and accommodate the outcome into your life. You experience creative exhaustion, but never the 'drama exhaustion' of a maneuvering, survival-based existence. You are in Love, energized and inspired to keep going every day. You are thriving!

CREATIVE EXPERIMENT

A great example of discerning flow was my attempt to create the right impact with my previous book *Thrive! Falling in Love with Life*. My partner Shirin and I hold a vision for it to reach the right readers – those who will truly be impacted and inspired by the book.

Conventional understanding (and free will) directed us to doing a press release, contacting bookstores, finding the right distribution channels...and we did all these things with due diligence. Immediately after the book's launch, in the direction of further life flow, I visited New York to train with my Guru in classical music. One of the other disciples of the music school had just read my book and was so deeply moved that she spontaneously organized a book reading and dialogue. Twenty-five people attended at short notice, and one of the attendees was moved enough to tell the Program Director of a television channel about *Thrive!* and about my short stay in the area. He, in turn, took one glance at the book's title and description, and decided that I should be interviewed for his television channel. When I stepped into the interview I was amazed to find the Program Director in perfect resonance with the content of the book. He asked me deeply meaningful questions, resulting in a wonderful interview.

All this happened in a matter of four or five days, and I was discombobulated by the whirlwind of events. It would have been easy to buckle under pressure and say I was unprepared, but I knew from the synchronicity of events that they were in the direction of flow, and I needed to align my free will with the flow as it was being revealed to me. I did the spiritual, emotional and physical hard labor to deliver – both at the book dialogue and at the interview, but the events themselves materialized without any organizing, managing or directing on my part.

Quickly in the heels of this, upon my return to Seattle, a creative (musical) collaboration with a friend materialized another book dialogue at the Kirkland Performance Center. From both the New York and Seattle-area events, people approached me organically to ask if I would coach or teach the insights in *Thrive!* It so happened that I had already run a pilot series of Creativity Workshops in the Fall of 2011, also organically conceived after I received repeated requests from participants of *Yoni ki Baat*, another collective creative endeavor that I had guided back in early 2011. Now, I was able to respond to these new requests with more rounds of Creativity Workshops in 2012, and turn the workshops into a laboratory of sorts for the practice of creativity. It is from these workshops that the impetus for this book emerged!

Shirin and I now realize that our vision to have *Thrive!*'s content touch lives did manifest, but *how* it manifested had its own flow, one governed by our joint higher purpose (- teaching is a significant aspect of mine and serving a part of hers-) and the Universe's specific need at the moment. Had we chosen solely out of free will, we would have continued to do press releases and to get *Thrive!* into various bookstores and so on...in general, focusing our efforts on increasing *readership* of the book rather than facilitating the *experience* of its content. By recognizing the flow of the moment, we aligned our free will with it, offering the insights in *Thrive!* in participatory, dynamic, interactive settings to tangibly impact lives. And from all this, another book is now being born within sixteen months!

8

SUMMON THE COSMIC LAUGH...

...EMBRACE UNCERTAINTY [YANG]

In the essay on Love in Chapter Two, I had referenced the quality of lightness in Love. I like to say that a cosmic laugh emanates when one has acquired enough perspective that one sees the humor in all of life, in every situation, no matter how challenging it is in the functional or operational sense. The feminine, Yin creative action is to stay connected with this cosmic laugh, the ability to find humor and light-heartedness in all that is, *just* the way it is.

Observe sometime how much the Dalai Lama grins and laughs! And of course, who hasn't noticed a baby's bright-eyed gurgles and giggles? This way of being in Light – both in the sense of illumination and in the sense of lightheartedness – is a very high-frequency, awakened state. It affords access to expanded awareness, always providing perspective and joy, allowing lots of room for silliness, and charting a return to our original, pure, childlike selves. From here we can create afresh, on a blank canvas.

This isn't just an attitude of making light of everything. Summoning the cosmic laugh is the ability to recognize how each turn of events is actually a creation in the direction of your spirit's natural flow. I call this lightheartedness 'cosmic' because it is, once again, related to one's connection with Spirit, with higher order flow, with the Universe's larger intent. It's like Spirit just cracked a gentle joke (always in the direction of your true soul purpose, and never in service of your ego's wants and needs), and is waiting to hear your response, whispering, "Get it? Get it?" If you're in expanded awareness, you're able to instantly recognize the joke and say,

"Aha! So *that's* how you're playing with me!" So, the joke is enjoyed in communion with Spirit. My sister tells me that the Germans have a saying that roughly translates to, "You can make God laugh by telling him your plans!"

The chuckles that inevitably emanate in such a humorous exchange also announce that 'Aha!' moment of recognition, the same as a stroke of genius in the creative process. I often find myself laughing out loud in awe in these moments of clarity and realization, and because laughter changes one's energy, I am immediately catapulted to a higher frequency. From here, what is created next is always in the direction of higher purpose, flow and Love. Comedian Chris Bliss says eloquently in an inspiring TEDex talk,[31]

"The alchemy of laughter turns our walls into windows, revealing a fresh and unexpected point of view."

Bliss also explains the process in physiological terms: Laughter releases endorphins in the brain, which lower our defenses (as opposed to anger or fear, which release adrenaline that erects walls). Whatever the actual process of alchemy may be, engaging the cosmic laugh immediately and

---

[31] Watch : http://tedxrainier.com/2/speaker_bliss.asp

invariably reveals new insight for me. As soon as I get the joke and begin to laugh, I am uplifted into a high frequency vibration with at least momentary access to pure, unmitigated awareness. In a rapid-fire slide show, new connections and insights about a situation, person or project reveal themselves, and I am instantaneously able to connect the dots for a creative approach in alignment with higher order flow.

Stay connected with Spirit's loving jokes! Humor has the unique ability to circumvent our ingrained perspectives and thought patterns, and make possible new ways of thinking and seeing, and ultimately, being and creating in the world.

9
SURRENDER YOUR ERRORS...
...FAIL OFTEN AND PUBLICLY [YANG]

A decidedly feminine creative action is to practice a constant, gentle acceptance of one's errors. I've known for a while that one cannot have compassion toward the world if one doesn't have it for oneself; so, holding forgiveness for one's own errors is necessary for loving the world better. But, an even deeper insight hit home recently. And that is, *surrender your error and it is no longer one!*

Now, how is that possible? Well, surrendering my error requires that I first recognize it as an error. Let's assume most of us reading this can do that most of the time. The typical pattern thereafter, however, often involves guilt, regret, self-blaming, or on the extreme side, self-flagellation and self-shaming. This is where one has quickly fallen from the initial, Love-based recognition that can lead to true creative insight, to the ego's judging, fear-based response. This berating voice says things like, "You should have known better! What will the world think of you?" Or it wants to rush to the apology. "I am sorry; please don't be angry with me!" In other words, "You, who I have wronged, please now also help me avoid the discomfort I am having to feel, by assuring me it's all okay!" None of this is in integrity with the initial high-frequency, awakened state of recognition of error. Instead, it is all about making oneself tall and proud once again, founded in the latent belief that the world should always think nothing but good of oneself, that error is 'wrong,' and so on.

Surrendering my error requires that upon recognizing it, I maintain the loving gaze upon myself to allow further intuitive inquiry, and *feel* the (sometimes excruciating) discomfort that arises from this process. Guilt, blame and shame may arise but they pass quickly...and then, I find, a powerful transmutation occurs. Suddenly the heaviness releases and there is understanding, revelation, light, Love, and even joy, inspiration and creativity from what has been uncovered. The error itself can then be given away – to the Universe, to Spirit, to the open skies or flowing river – whatever metaphor suits you well. Combine it with the cosmic laugh, and now the error becomes one more act of revelation and creation that *actually puts me back on the right path*. What appeared like a wrong turn, is on the right path after all! Love deepens, and if an apology is still warranted, it is loving, meaningful and timely. So, suddenly, the error is not an error anymore. It is, instead, a quantum leap on the right path!

What happens when I *don't* do this? When I cling to ego's voice telling me that I should've known better? Or, if only I had done this or thought of that? Well, then I'm back on the wrong path; or rather, I'm scurrying about madly on the guilt-shame-blame treadmill that leads nowhere at all but the dead, dead-end.

Once in a while, I see a clear vision of the illusion of multiple paths. Right, wrong, right, left...when in fact, just like time, in which past, present and future can all be conflated to the single point of Now, in this vision, all seemingly divergent paths converge into one single thick strand – like a multi-layered highway – that we're all walking on, returning home to our truths. To experience this sense of no-wrong-path, one must constantly surrender one's errors and move with higher order flow.

In both projects and in life, errors are little windows for quantum leaps. Errors can put us back on the right path – the creative, generative path. Surrendering one's errors, therefore, is the key to a creative existence, and a significant responsibility of the feminine, Yin principle.

CREATIVE EXPERIMENT

Creativity Workshop participant Pallavi Garg, who creates through technology strategies, poetry, visual art and craft, finds that glass bead-making is routinely an opportunity to practice surrendering her errors. When she misses a step in the process or doesn't prepare adequately, she can't really create the effect she's after. The feelings of frustration upon realizing her error can at times snowball into making the bead a lost cause. But when Pallavi regards the error with gentleness, she immediately recognizes other possibilities that exist alongside her original vision for the bead. And magically, the bead takes form, shape and color as its own unique self.

10
NURTURE THE SEEDLING...
...SHARE THE FRUIT [YANG]

So far we've explored employing the feminine, Yin principle to cultivate in all sorts of ways – listening in stillness, preparing a womb, building support and community, allowing the Muse to channel through, and allowing synchronicity and flow to guide us along the way. What about when the creation has just sprung forth in form? Is there an appropriate role for the Yin energy at this stage and beyond?

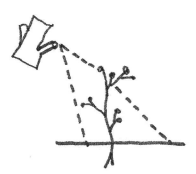

Like a mother tending to her young-one, the Yin principle has a valuable contribution to make in the early stages of the birth of an idea, when the seed has just sprouted into the seedling. While this youngling must interact with the elements – for it needs sun, water and air to nourish it into a plant – too much heat or wind or storm, and the seedling can perish. The loving feminine creative action here is to construct just enough porosity around the creative seedling so that it receives nourishment from the elements – from all the enriching audience interactions it must have and from all the public failing it will benefit from – while also having adequate protection to continue its growth into the plant it is meant to be.

One of the most significant discoveries I've made while practicing this action is to stumble upon the difference between feedback and co-creation. As far as I am concerned, feedback is just what it sounds like – reactive regurgitation. Are you shocked? Amused? I now have very little value for feedback unless it is of the straightforward kind such as, "Hey, it really hurts my arm when you press that way!" *That* is useful feedback. Everything else is pretty much useless because it puts me in a position to react to someone else's personal preferences, reactions or speculations, rather than allowing a creative act to emerge organically in integrity with its inherent DNA. At worst, it causes downward-spiral thinking based in reactivity and fear.

Co-creation is very different. In a co-creative process, those you share with offer responses like, "That particular aspect really resonates with me!" Or, "This made me curious to understand more..." Or, "Hey, what if you did this...?" In the Creativity Workshops I facilitate, participants co-create in colleagues' presentations in exactly this way. All responses to a presentation *must* begin with, "What pops for me is...," or "I wonder...," or "What if...?" These types of observations and questions are significantly different from feedback, energetically and otherwise. They are invaluable insights on the inherent nature of the creation that you, as the creative channel, may not be able to see. So, others are becoming mirrors in your creative process and providing you reflections that allow you to nurture, build, and grow. They are creating possibility. They are providing just the right environment for the plant or tree to be the fullest, most glorious manifestation it can be. And if the original idea is really not substantial, then the reflections offered will organically guide you to a new idea, without ever killing anything – your idea or your spirit.

The art of the feminine creative principle is to discern the difference between feedback and co-creation, and consciously immerse in environments and support systems that provide the latter. I always recognize co-creation by the fact that the interaction expands possibility rather than causing a downward spiral based in reactivity or fear. And of course I feel the energy in my body. This discernment is a delicate balancing act, and as always, any delicate action in the creative cycle is best served by the powerful intuition of the feminine principle.

4

OUTER ACTION

THE CREATIVE YANG

"You can learn all you want about Freud, but sooner or later you have to go out with the girls."

– Wallace Andrews

"The legs are the wheels of creativity."

– Albert Einstein

"If you have built castles in the air, your work need not be lost; that is where they should be. Now put the foundations under them."

– Henry David Thoreau

1

MEDITATE [YIN]

... MOVE

The one-word action that best represents the masculine or Yang principle of creativity is: Move! Moving is about generating by 'going through the motions,' whether physically or intellectually, but more often than not, focused on the former.

If meditating in physical stillness is one way to channel the Muse, then movement is its physically expressive complement. Going through the motions using the skills, tools or resources related to a creative expression even without being visited by the 'big idea' is a powerful way of exercising creativity. Simply developing a skill or craft – singing to exercise the voice, dancing to music with no aim, shaving something down in a woodshop, moving a brush with no artistic concept in mind, playing with Lego or putty, or even doing physical labor or chores – does wonders for exercising your creative ability when done joyfully, even when such movement is apparently aimless and separate from creative intention on a particular project. Almost always, showing up to do the work anyway – to exercise the creative muscle – actually gives birth to the creative idea.

For instance, an incredible discovery I made along these lines is that I can best absorb the essence of a Raga, a melodic scale in Indian classical music, if I listen to my class recordings while moving my brush on canvas! This doesn't preclude the hard work required, such as doing the actual musical exploration involved in learning the Raga. Still, listening to instruction while my body is moving and doing something else encourages a different learning and understanding, not otherwise available to me by meeting the material head-on. And my painting gets richer for it too! My hand moves in ways to the music that it may not do when I follow predetermined ideas for how the painting should unfold. Suddenly, I have two creative products from one integrated exercise – merely of movement.

Movement for the sake of movement, when done joyfully, is powerful because it allows us to get out of our own way, and creates an empty space similar to the one meditative stillness does. It also allows actual physical energy to begin flowing. The Muse receives an invitation to show up as part of the flow through the empty space. In addition, the movement hones the skill or craft in question, making it more and more possible for the expression to actually flow through into tangible product, when the Muse does visit.

Every practice I enlist hereafter in this chapter is some specific variant of moving that cultivates creativity in rich and significant ways. Like everything else, intentional movement is a loving action. It creates positive energy ripples in the environment, the precursor to full creative action.

2

EMPTY YOURSELF FOR STILLNESS [YIN]

...JUST DO IT, JUST TO DO IT

If emptying yourself for creative stillness is the feminine principle necessary for cultivating a receptive womb for the Muse, then its masculine counterpoint is *Just Do It, Just To Do It*! The Yang principle is activated every time we take outward creative action in the world – move energy, become physical, speak up, stand up for something, generate, organize, connect, and so on.

One of the biggest challenges creatives face when taking action is hearing the persistent chatter of rational thought, which is also an aspect of the masculine principle, but it can be at odds with creative action if it originates from fear and doubt. This voice plagues us with pesky questions like, "Why should I do this?" "Is there really any value?" "What will the outcome be?" "What are the risk factors?" "Can it really be manufactured?" "What if people hate it?" "Will there be an ROI?" On and on – by now you know the voice of fear and resistance well!

As I've alluded to before, rational thought can often be just another clever disguise of fear. In his teachings on the emergence of your innate soul blueprint, Derek Rydall terms the crippling nature of this kind of rationalization within the creative process as "premature practicality."[32] The valuable purpose of rational thought is to *serve* us in successful execution and implementation of an intuitive creative insight, not to heavily evaluate or judge its worthiness in the first

---

[32] Listen to Derek Rydall's Soul Purpose Blueprint audio series at http://yoursoulpurposeblueprint.com

place. This subtle difference is so immensely significant that it can make or break the creative. It is the difference between the one who consistently gets creative work out there and the other who sits paralyzed in her chair dreaming up big ideas, but never starts or finishes anything, all in the name of perfection, whether it is the perfect timing, situation, resources, expected outcome, and so on.

As discussed previously, perfectionism is one of the cleverest and most dangerous masquerades of fear, because it pretends to add value – after all, we think 'perfect' is best! But perfectionism is rational, critical thought on steroids, entirely crippling and debilitating any creative action. I'm even inclined to agree with the idea that perfectionism is the enemy of excellence.

The way to circumvent paralyzing rational thought and perfectionism is to *Just Do It, Just To Do It*, once creative stillness has intuitively revealed the glimpse of a potential path. Nike's most brilliant contribution to the world is their tagline, *Just Do It*. In those three simple words lies the incredible empowerment available to the athlete (or any creative) – the choice to just go for it. To take that leap of faith, to take flight.

When I witness creatives through their efforts, I add a subtle but important little extension to Nike's original clarion call – *Just To Do It*. This portion of the call represents the freedom from attachment to outcome that must accompany the doing. This means that once a potential path has revealed itself, once the Muse has whispered to you, creative action must be taken with faith, Love and joy, with an inner knowing that the outcome will be just right even if it is imperfect.

So, *Just Do It, Just To Do It* means taking creative action for no other reason than its inherent value, for the purity of doing it. For no other reason than because it is loving, because it gives you joy, because it lifts your energy. Because it enriches your time with the feeling of utter exhilaration, or better still, because time stops still and you completely lose yourself while doing it. The creative process *is* the product; the journey *is* the destination!

As Steven Pressfield says in his compelling book *Do the Work*, "Start before you're ready." Just Do It, Just To Do It!

3
EXPAND YOUR AWARENESS [YIN]
...AND DO IT DAILY!

While the feminine principle of working from expanded or pure awareness is being cultivated, the masculine principle can be complementarily exercised by the disciplined action of *daily* doing, without question or exception.

There is something amazing to be said for showing up to do the work every single day, at the appointed time, come rain or sunshine, feel like it or not. Many creative people have written about and have outlined in detail, their methods for accomplishing this daily, ritualistic attendance. Dancer and choreographer Twyla Tharp does it by hailing a cab at 5:30am and taking herself to the gym, no matter what, every single day. She "likes it warm," and as a dancer, warmth in her body is the very fuel of her creative existence. Steven Pressfield talks about sitting down every day to write for a fixed amount of hours (no greater and no fewer), always at the same time of day, and without holiday the entire year.

Serial entrepreneur Tim Ferris speaks of keeping at bay for the first four hours of the day, all external information (such as news, email, etc.) to ensure that he produces his own creative output on a fresh and empty mind, every single day. (In fact, he has enjoyed a period in his life when he managed to banish email to once a week!) And in Elizabeth Gilbert's famous TED talk that I've referenced twice before, she describes how day after day of her showing up like a "mule" enables her "brushing up" against the Muse on certain days, always unexpectedly. Her job and ours, Gilbert maintains, is "to have the sheer human Love and stubbornness to keep showing up."

I have a strong sense that the daily doing is the Yang complement to the Yin action of cultivating expanded or pure awareness not so much because of its discipline or regularity or punctuality or even rigor, but because of its *ritualistic* nature. Twyla Tharp speaks of this as significant because rituals are performed without question and without exception. In my experience, this daily, unquestioned doing is valuable because it requires a state of surrender – the suspension of fear, mind, doubt, and questioning – paradoxically, opening one to genuine curiosity and inquiry through generative activity. It returns one to a childlike purity, which is why ancient cultures used rituals for 'purification.' Such surrender therefore enables access to expanded awareness, and calls it powerfully into play in one's creativity. The Muse blesses and visits your ritualistic doing because you have surrendered in purity, and can now better listen and channel her faithfully into creative action.

The legendary Pandit Jasraj, my Guru's Guru of Hindustani Classical Music, said to me recently in an interview of him that I was conducting on behalf of two international collaborators documenting the transcendental experiences of musicians and dancers across the world,[33] *"Karata karata abhyas jadamati hota sujan."* This roughly translates from Hindi as, "Daily practice awakens (even) the wisdom of stone." So, even something as inert, hard and lifeless as stone can become 'wise' from showing up every day, from surrender to daily, unquestioned, ritualistic doing.

CREATIVE EXPERIMENT

For Creativity Workshop participant Sudha Nandagopal, *Just Do It*, *Just To Do It*, and *Do It Daily* have been her mantras in the complete recreation of her body over the year 2012. Previously, she had struggled with when to work out, how to eat healthily, if she had enough energy, and so on. This time around, she adopted the mentality of *Just Do It*, focusing on one day at a time – simply getting up and doing the work. On most days, working out was the first thing she did. She also stopped constantly weighing herself and followed her trainer's advice, "Trust the work and your

---

[33] The working title of this book, not yet published at the time of this writing, is *Inner Experiences*.

body will respond." As long as Sudha was stressing about not seeing changes, the changes were stuck. As soon as she let go of timelines and measurements, and just focused on showing up every day and making working out a priority, her body and health transformed. All of this happened not in a year when she had a lot of extra time or energy, but in the most challenging of years for her career. Sudha reached her best physical health in years, fulfilling a decade-long promise to herself, and setting herself up for a healthy winter and a great international trip.

4

RECOGNIZE SYNCHRONICITY [YIN]

...CONNECT THE DOTS

If recognizing synchronicity is a Yin principle of creative action, then actively connecting the dots is the corresponding Yang aspect.

One of my most favorite short-and-sweet definitions of creativity is: *Creativity is connecting the dots in ways unique to you*. In fact, in my consulting work in design strategy I have often said of myself in project proposals: *Dot Connector par excellence*! Quite seriously, if I were given a choice to list only *one* skill of mine that rises to the top, I'd say it is the ability to rapidly connect the dots in unique and meaningful ways when faced with a sea of seemingly unrelated information and experiences. Many a CEO or big-picture thinker will tell you the same thing – they seem to see meaningful connections where others wouldn't. As Steve Jobs, one of my biggest creative heroes, famously said in a *Wired* Magazine interview in 1995 titled *The Next Insanely Great Thing*:[34]

"Creativity is just connecting things. When you ask creative people how they did something, they feel a little guilty because they didn't really do it, they just saw something. It seemed obvious to them after a while. That's because they were able to connect experiences they've had, and synthesize new things... A lot of people...haven't had very diverse experiences. So they don't have enough dots to connect...The broader one's understanding of the human experience, the better design we will have."

In *Brain Pickings*, Maria Popova discusses what she calls "the combinatorial aspect of creativity." She profiles the book *Dancing About Architecture: A Little Book of Creativity* by Phil Beadle,[35] and points out how he emphasizes this combinatorial aspect. Popova quotes Beadle:

"The mind, at its best, is a pattern-making machine, engaged in a perpetual attempt to impose order on to chaos; making links between disparate entities or ideas in order to better understand either or both. It is the ability to spot the potential in the product of connecting things that don't ordinarily go together that marks out the person who is truly creative."

Connecting the dots seems as ancient an instinct as one significant to the pre-historic hunter-gatherer, who needed to scan a landscape very quickly to gain insight into where food may be found, how dangerous the prospect is, and how to get the most out of the least risk. As Twyla Tharp

---

[34] See: http://www.wired.com/wired/archive/4.02/jobs_pr.html

[35] See: http://www.brainpickings.org/index.php/2012/04/27/dancing-about-architecture-phil-beadle/

writes, this action is also closely tied with another function of survival – our memory, wherein we store away important facts, fictions and feelings from our experiences, and later connect them to make meaning.

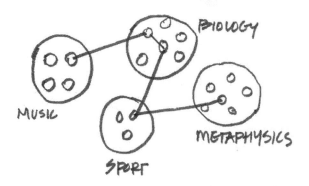

While all this makes connecting the dots sound like a survival instinct, a higher-order version of it is a way to thrive in creativity. In this higher-order version, it becomes the art of using metaphor to convey Truth that achieves timeless relevance. Tharp writes,

"Metaphor is the lifeblood of all art, if it's not the art itself."

This ability to connect the dots into metaphor isn't just an innate talent, though some people are much better at it than others. It is a cultivated practice, a constant creative action, which gets better with the number of times you head out to hunt and gather! As Steve Jobs suggests, constantly broadening our life experiences and observation skills allows us to practice scanning the landscape, and connecting the dots in meaningful ways into metaphors of timeless value.

In the spiritual version of this skill, connecting the dots becomes the ability to scan the signs, messages and frequencies that we see, hear and sense when we are in synchronicity with the higher intelligence and flow of the Universe, and then connect the dots to discover *guidance* for oneself and for creating one's life. In this way, this skill serves the deepening internal understanding of unfolding Truth, and brings forth authentic external creative action.

5

INVITE, ENROLL AND PREPARE TO RECEIVE [YIN]

...CONTRIBUTE TO A POSITIVE SUM GAME

If inviting and enrolling others into a community of creatives is a Yin action, then its complementary Yang practice is to always be a contribution. In particular, this is expressed in the confident knowing that every creative idea you freely offer up is only going to come back to you richer and stronger.

In *The Art of Possibility*, Ben Zander and Rosamund Stone Zander dedicate a whole chapter to 'being a contribution.' They describe how, unlike comparative and evaluative terms like success or failure, contribution has no other side. Asking oneself every day, "How will I be a contribution today?" is always a win-win proposition. To practice being a contribution, the Zanders recommend that you "throw yourself into life as someone who makes a difference, accepting that you may not understand how or why." What this means is that just by the mere act of fully being in your life and genuinely caring about the world, you are *already* a contribution. This way of interacting with and giving to the world is a faith- and Love-inspired action. It is the alignment of one's free will in the direction of Universal good.

An important aspect of being a contribution and relinquishing old, fear-based measurement and evaluation models, is to completely let go of constructs of authorship. While it is still important to practice integrity and gratitude in crediting others for their ideas, the concept of singular authorship, copyrights and patents is an old-world idea that is going to die in our new world of connected consciousness. In the new, Love-inspired world of creativity as sole human purpose, each of us is known as a limitless wellspring of ideas who is never, ever going to run out of this abundance. Additionally, while one may be the individual channel for the Muse, each of us is channeling Universal intelligence, which belongs to all of us and none of us. We cannot patent Spirit any more than we can patent the oxygen we breathe!

So, when you're visited by Spirit in your imagination and freely gifted ideas, protect less and give more! Freely give away your ideas; you know that you're probably not going to build on all of them, anyway. I find that sharing ideas begets more ideas, not only because they multiply synergistically when offered to other co-creators, but also because when my own internal pipeline of ideas is kept in motion and flow, I get a more continuous supply of ideas from Spirit – that is, I am more inspired!

The happy corollary to giving away ideas is to freely 'steal' them. Build on other people's ideas, because this is how you love, honor and celebrate them, and expand humanity's collective potential. In the little gem of a book, *Steal Like An Artist*, Austin Kleon makes the case that there is no such thing as an original idea, and that your originality is essentially your way of seeing the same thing someone else saw differently. And he insists that it is actually our responsibility to 'steal' generously! In a simple list, Kleon outlines the differences between 'good theft' and 'bad theft.' In good theft, a Love-based endeavor, we honor, study, credit, remix or transform what we've stolen. In bad theft, an undoubtedly fear-based exercise, we degrade, skim, plagiarize, imitate or rip off from someone. In good theft we also steal from many and connect the dots uniquely to make new meaning. In bad theft we're just lazily taking something from one person without adding any Love of our own to it.

By both giving away and stealing lovingly and generously, we keep the Universe in flow with ideas, and contribute like it's always a positive sum game. In doing so, individual and human creativity at large are exponentially expanded.

6
CHANNEL THE MUSE THROUGH [YIN]
...SCULPT AWAY THE DEBRIS

If channeling the Muse through is a Yin action, then its corresponding Yang action is to commit to chipping away the excess stone to reveal the sculpture, both within our physical medium for creative action, and within ourselves. This conscious, dedicated and disciplined action is all about ensuring that one's conditioning and programming don't run interference with the essence of the idea that is channeling through us. This idea is Michelangelo's brilliant observation; he knew that he is but the servant freeing the sculpture already hidden within the block of marble with which he is working. And this is also the very premise of this book! The true, creative you is simply sitting obscured within layers of false conditioning, and will reveal itself as you exercise your creativity in the playground of material reality. Your creations will in turn create you!

The DNA of a creative act, product, interaction or movement is set when intention meets possibility, at the time of conception – in that mysterious moment of interaction between human heart and Universal intelligence, when the Muse strikes. Thereafter, all outer creative action must focus on serving this innate blueprint, and executing its full formal expression. This is not unlike rearing a child or nurturing a love relationship. A child is her own person, and as a parent, one's responsibility is best served by being as much of a loving *witness* to this awesome emergence as possible, while providing for basic, survival needs as long as necessary. A love relationship also has its unique DNA located in the space of I-and-Thou, about which the philosopher Martin Buber has written so beautifully. To recognize this special DNA and align all action to serve it, leads to a growing, thriving and fulfilling relationship, including determining when it must transform to a new and different equation.

The other implication of seeing creative action as an act of sculpting is that one focuses more on editing than on augmenting. As the famous (but not-so-unequivocally attributed) quote goes, "If I had more time, I would have written a shorter letter." Writing the shorter letter requires not only the time, but the disciplined ability to recognize the essence and integrity of the idea, the Muse just as it is channeling through, and doing *only* the work that is necessary and appropriate in serving it. It is the act of writing the short story with the long line, as discussed in Chapter Two. The subtle challenge is figuring out how to move one's ego, which shows up as opinion, analysis, identity, or self-consciousness, out of the way, and allow the idea to take form true to its own innate essence.

I can best explain this by citing examples from the way my poetry or visual art unfolds. Each poem that channels through me often initially arrives not as one big idea, but in a few disparate, distinct phrases. It's literally as if these phrases are visiting me out of the blue, and I must find the connections between them to *discover* the poem that is emerging! This often involves faithfully recording these phrases out of turn even if they make no sense to me individually or together, until I see a larger pattern or connection emerge. It is only then that I might 'tame' the phrases into some sort of poetic form or meter and all those good structural devices, but the essence of the poem, like a child that comes forth into this world, arrives intact with its innate DNA. It's up to me to recognize this blueprint, channel it through, and connect the dots into meaning, all with the lightest touch possible.

My painting ideas, on the other hand, often arrive as conceptual wholes. I usually draw these up as large, abstract, generic scaffolds. When I actually fill in the scaffold with color, the painting completes itself. In so filling in, I must take care that the colors, brush strokes and other choices I make are in integrity with the DNA of the central idea that has channeled through me. The same is true for an architectural design; I must ensure that my follow-through in terms of material details is free of stylistic preconception, and that as far as possible, the idea maintains its integrity independent of the personal preferences that may have been conditioned into me. This is, of course, only possible to a certain extent, because the hand that draws is going to have its imprint on the idea. My main point is simply that this imprint must be as light, and as much in service of the essential idea as possible.

This act of sculpting away the debris is the ultimate in unconditionally loving service. In doing so, one is transformed and truly revealed by one's own creation, rather than the other way around. I've often remarked while writing this book, that *this book is writing me*!

CREATIVE EXPERIMENT

Creativity Workshop participant Kamal Janardhan is a new mother, and has just returned to work as a Program Manager in a large, global corporation, at the time of this writing. Recently, she was working on a presentation deck every night, furiously creating a buttress against every possible attack and argument. One night, as she was working, she was reminded of the principles taught in the Creativity Workshop due to a serendipitous online run-in with one of her co-participants. They spoke about how they can both approach every workplace conversation with curiosity and a desire to understand, rather than a wish to vanquish. In other words, Kamal became prepared to *be a contribution* through her efforts at re-integrating into her new leadership role at work, as well as move her smaller self – her fear-driven buttressing efforts – out of the way, thereby *sculpting away the debris*. Miraculously, her baby fell asleep without a feed that night, and in subsequent days, she was able to (re)create several conversations and presentations at work into supportive dialogues that expanded or created new possibility for all.

7

DISTINGUISH FREE WILL FROM FLOW [YIN]

...MAKE DISCONTINUOUS, QUANTUM LEAPS

If recognizing flow and intuitively discerning it apart from free will is the feminine principle's responsibility, then putting that free will into the right external action in alignment with higher order flow, is the complementary responsibility of the masculine principle. As discussed in the previous essay *Sculpt Away the Debris*, this often involves stepping out of one's own way, which means taking one's ego, personality or conditioning out of the way, and also learning how to reveal and edit rather than augment all the time.

A significant aspect of enacting free will in alignment with higher order flow is the ability to make discontinuous, quantum leaps. This means spotting the wormholes and traveling them rather than remaining slave to notions of linear and sequential process or journey. It means knowing when and how to transform from the state of caterpillar to that of butterfly, with the unexplained, mysterious phenomenon of imaginal cells in between. The opportunities to circumvent linear time-oriented process only become visible to us if we've sufficiently practiced stillness and recognizing Universal flow. Some notable characteristics of these opportunities to travel wormholes are that they seem synchronous and 'unbelievable' or 'too good to be true' to the rational mind, they are game-changing, they sometimes involve a wholesale quitting action from the path one is currently on, and they afford very short-range visibility on how it's all going to work out. In other words, they scare the daylights out of you!

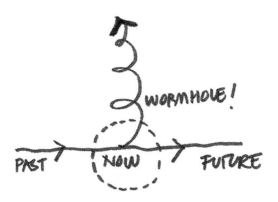

In Chapter Two I discussed transcending the myth of process or journey. The typical notion is that everything is a step-by-step process, rooted in time-based beliefs in linearity and sequence. When one is no longer entrenched in these beliefs (reserving them entirely for operational purposes in material reality), and has begun to recognize the Universe's higher order flow and synchronicity, it becomes evident that there are leaps one can make that are not literally progressive or evolutionary, but often lateral or completely discontinuous. Such moves might even appear like complete non-sequiturs. And often they catapult one into a completely different playing field, in which the paradigm and rules are brand new, a discontinuous state from the previous one.

For instance, in the creative experiment regarding the promotion of my previous book *Thrive!*, a quantum leap meant skipping all promotion activity on the book and beginning to facilitate Creativity Workshops instead, which in turn led unexpectedly to the material for this book in very short order. This catapulting from book to book would not have happened so rapidly had I been following the conventional journey after a book publication, or not listening for the signs that showed me what the higher order flow was revealing.

Another example that I've referenced before is about the unexpected leap I made in my Indian classical singing, when I stopped practicing something that was eluding me for months, and sang easier pieces for a while. Then, I had the complex composition that had thus far eluded me, playing in the background while working on a large visual art piece. The physical motion of the brush and paints combined with listening to the tapes must have done something to short-circuit my old brain patterns. One minute I didn't know how to sing the composition properly in its rhythm cycle, and another minute I did. There was no linear time in between – I'd made a discontinuous, discrete, instantaneous jump. I'm sure I would have eventually learned to sing the composition correctly with conventional, hard-earned practice the way classical music stalwarts recommend, but I had made a leap with very little time investment in that moment, by allowing higher order flow to take care of things. And I had a new painting finished to boot, which in turn, had undoubtedly benefitted from the music! Thus started my practice of making visual art while listening to an Indian classical Raga. It allows me to get out of the way of both things – the music and the art – and become instead, a channel for the higher order to flow through. My free will aligns with this flow, and creation simply creates itself!

Making these discontinuous leaps is an act of unconditional Love because, of course, you have to let go of the old and trust the new without question or condition.

CREATIVE EXPERIMENT

My partner in the creativity platform Flying Chickadee, Shirin Subhani, often talks about how much leaping we constantly do – every single month – with our monthly magazine *Courageous Creativity*. It all started when we were beginning to receive interest from independent writers who had ideas or even drafts for books, but weren't ready to jump into publishing yet. We, however, weren't up to waiting to become a venue for collective creativity. So, we asked ourselves: Why not curate intentional collections of short works? And we leaped! Within a month, we were working on the first issue of *Courageous Creativity*. Neither of us had done any work with a magazine before, and we weren't sure how to source our contributors. We only had our vision, our faith, our talents and skills, and our perseverance. And we had our connections with many other courageous and creative people.

Sure enough, month after month, all we have really had to do is choose a theme, hold the intention, invite and enroll, and then be ready and willing to receive, do the work and then share the fruit! Month after month, we leap, simply holding the faith that the right contributors will show up, and show up they do. Every month, eight amazing storytellers from all over the world respond to our invitations, become our co-creators, and together we develop and launch a beautiful issue each time.

In the early months we had started out by inviting people we knew, people who seemed approachable and people with great stories of courage, creativity and change and a willingness to share. Somewhere along the way, we made the next leap to ask people who seemed unreachable, people you read about or watch on TV or TED talks. We found that they appreciated very much that we had invited them, loved our magazine's vision, and easily became co-creators. *Courageous Creativity* has made several leaps in the three years and more than thirty issues it has completed!

8

SUMMON THE COSMIC LAUGH [YIN]

...EMBRACE UNCERTAINTY

If discerning the difference between free will and flow is the feminine, Yin principle in action, then externally embracing and even actively inviting uncertainty into one's life and creative process is the complementary masculine, Yang action. Ever since giving up the illusion of control for nearly a decade now, I've discovered that in embracing uncertainty lies an immense opening to creativity. In zooming far, far out of the apparent entropy and chaos, I see dots I can connect, meaning I can make, and visions I can realize. Uncertainty has become the only certain thing in my life! I like to be very aware and watchful of comfort, especially the kind that sneaks in attachment. The moment something becomes comfortable in a status quo sort of way, I know it's time to actively push myself to the space of uncertainty.

It might appear that actively being in uncertainty is some kind of willful tempting of fate or an intentional jeopardizing of one's safety and security. Not at all! If anything, it is a relinquishing of the illusion of certainty, recognizing that there is no such thing in the first place, and reshaping one's consciousness to remain in the truth and limitless possibility of uncertainty. Paradoxically, with practice, it is uncertainty that becomes genuinely comforting, because you are always in the space of all possibility! This is not to be confused with a lack of commitment in a greedy bid to keep all options open. Rather, it is a focused, committed doing without attachment to certain outcomes over others.

Why is actively embracing or inviting uncertainty into one's process so significant to creativity? Dennis Merritt Jones, author of *The Art of Uncertainty: How to Live in the Mystery of Life and Love it*, explains that nothing new can be created from the field of what we already know, and therefore, stepping into the mystery of the unknown is the only way to become a conscious co-creator of life. Earlier in the book, I've referenced my favorite teaching of Einstein, which says that no solution can be created by the same consciousness that originated the problem. Einstein and Jones are pointing to the insight that the field of infinite possibility opens up only when we make a concerted effort to remain in uncertainty.

Another way I explore this idea is through Heisenberg's uncertainty principle, which describes the behavior of a quantum system. The principle states that the momentum and location of a particle cannot be simultaneously predicted. In spiritual terms the uncertainty principle suggests to me that the act of observing something[36] in a particular way is likely to create it in our material reality in *that* particular way, leaving its other possibility states un-manifested (or unseen). This further reveals to me that viewing something with certainty can be an act of creating but *one* possibility of something. Remaining open to uncertainty, then, is the equivalent to expanding the number of possibility

---

[36] I understand that scientifically speaking, the uncertainty principle should not be confused with the observer effect, which states that a system cannot be observed or measured without affecting it.

states that can be created, and allowing higher order flow to reveal and guide which one(s) are right for that moment in time in the Universal system. Practicing in this way invariably allows for the most powerful and impactful possibility state to be created – something that is transformative and game-changing – a quantum leap.

Take, for instance, the uncertainty state of either a newly forming romantic relationship, or a turbulent one poised for a breakup – something probably familiar to one and all. In either of these situations, many of us become hungry for instant answers, eager for clarity to come quickly and efficiently. We want so badly to know, one way or another. "What potential does this thing have?" "Does she love me too?" "Is he going to leave me?"

Elevating oneself from this kind of contracted state of attachment and into expanded awareness, you are able to see that potential is always unlimited, and that there is no single outcome to any situation, no matter what the circumstances may be. (In fact, in pure awareness you see that there is no problem to begin with!) If it isn't in-the-face obvious that "She loves me," staying in the uncertainty actually expands the number of possibility states that can manifest. Being comfortably in the space of not-knowing enlarges the canvas, and suddenly, all sorts of possibility states enter the map between the two extremes of "She loves me" and "She loves me not." These could be "She doesn't know yet," "She is in the process of discovery," "She loves me and is also happy with advancing things at the pace they are now," "She loves me and she is content with her life as it is right now," and so on. In this larger space of uncertainty, were one to contract into focusing constantly on one's worst fear, "She doesn't love me," chances are rather high that one will *create* that very fear into existence! This is what is meant by a self-fulfilling prophecy; it is the creation of the very thing that one focuses on as if it were already created. It's what Henry Ford meant when he quipped,

> "If you think you can do it, or if you think you can't do it, you are right!"

While maintaining stillness in the face of uncertainty may seem like the feminine principle in action, embracing uncertainty is discussed as a Yang principle because I am referring to actively, intentionally and consistently putting oneself in the field of uncertainty. Get out there – poke, forage, risk! Repeatedly practice this uniquely masculine principle of exploring without guarantees.

CREATIVE EXPERIMENT

When Dharini Vasudevan joined the Creativity Workshops, she was in a place of great uncertainty. She was new to the United States and Seattle, still unemployed, and unsure of what she was doing here and where to go next, including what kind of jobs to apply for, if at all. Dharini boldly used the workshops to make *herself* the project. She fully embraced the uncertainty of her situation, putting aside her worries about the future, and began to dutifully and faithfully practice all the principles being taught. In fact, she took it to the highest extreme we've witnessed through the workshops, making every exercise central to her daily life. Her concluding project showcased herself as a person who is poised to allow whatever wants to emerge *through* her, to come to the world as service. Within a month of the workshops concluding, Dharini landed a position with the Human Resources division of a local software giant, specifically, their *Services* division. Thereafter, within the remaining year, she received opportunities to perform in a dance ensemble, publish her poetry, learn music and astrology, as well as attend an advanced meditation retreat. By embracing uncertainty, her life flowed in what she agrees are discontinuous, quantum jumps!

9

SURRENDER YOUR ERRORS [YIN]

...FAIL OFTEN AND PUBLICLY!

If surrendering one's errors is the Yin principle in action, then the complementary Yang principle is to fail often and publicly! An extension of the previous practice of embracing uncertainty – of foraging and risking, of seeking without knowing – is that one will probably fail often, and fail publicly.

That said, I'm not talking merely about failing as a natural by-product of taking risks. Like actively seeking out uncertainty, I am actually referring to cultivating the habit of intentional failure, and doing so publicly. (If you think about it, failing in private is somewhat like not failing at all!) How weird, you might say. Why must I fail if things are going smoothly? What is the creative advantage? Well, as Seth Godin says in an interview on *Behind The Brand*,[37]

"If I fail more often than you do, I win."

Godin explains that while playing, if you keep failing in a way that you still get to keep playing, eventually you'll succeed in some big way. The ones who don't succeed are those who never fail, or fail so big that they don't get to keep playing, which probably means that they didn't fail often enough along the way. The way I see it, failing often and publicly just means intentionally engaging the audience you've enrolled to become co-creators and pathfinders along with you. Each time your idea, product or conversation interacts with a caring, invested audience, especially when you're ready

---

[37] Watch: http://mashable.com/2011/12/07/seth-godin-video/

enough with your creation to share it but it's still cooking enough to be edited or augmented meaningfully through this interaction, you come away with your idea either grown or thrown away. And if it's the latter, then you're guaranteed something new born in place of what just retired. In this way, the act of failing publicly becomes an integral part of the continuous, iterative creative process. There is no 'me' and 'them' in failing in this way, because it's now 'we' creating together. I like to say that it's a fail-proof way of failing!

An important caveat for this practice is to make sure that one is never putting the audience in the role of approval-giver or decision-maker. They are your co-creators, not approvers or validators. If you're seeking approval, then you're unwilling to take responsibility, unwilling to fail. So, this is not the spirit of the engagement. While the interaction might serve as a vetting opportunity for an innovation, the ultimate call for whether a creation of yours is worthy of seeing the light of day must always and no matter what come from within you and your sacred interaction with Spirit, from the higher order flow of the Universe. What has channeled through you must come forth into the world because it has inherent value. If it resonates with you, if it makes your soul smile and your heart sing, if it inspires a dance in your step and raises your frequency, it is cause enough to birth it! In the spirit of failing publicly, what's the worst that will happen? It will fail, and it will fail publicly. And you will have unearthed something that makes your next creative endeavor that much better, while also having smiled and sung and danced through it all!

CREATIVE EXPERIMENT

At the conclusion of the Creativity Workshops, participant Arathi Srikantaiah successfully launched her health and nutrition Web site *Health Edited*, and then also published an article about it in the magazine *Courageous Creativity*. But then she found fear of failure keeping her from sharing her article on social media platforms or in other venues, thinking she is "a commoner," and would fail in providing anything of value to the world. In spite of her vast knowledge and generous spirit in creating what she had, she didn't feel confident about being a contribution. When Arathi finally shared her article on Facebook, she began instantly receiving messages of gratitude and congratulations, along with also receiving inquiries, ideas and pointers that rapidly shaped her next educational posts, recipes, and tools. Now, continuing with the practice of 'failing publicly,' she is finding that her readers are helping to shape *Health Edited*, and she is also beginning to feel an overwhelming sense of gratitude for and confidence in her unique place in the world.

10
NURTURE THE SEEDLING [YIN]
...SHARE THE FRUIT

If it is the Yin principle's responsibility to nurture the seedling, then to complement, the Yang principle must share the fruit! This sharing of creative outcomes with others –

audiences, readers, friends and family – is an absolutely essential part of the creative cycle.

While, previously, I've discussed interacting with audiences who've been enrolled as co-creators within the creative process, this particular practice is all about sharing for the sake of sharing, to spread the joy and Love. That by doing so one is still continuing to enroll audiences in the act of co-creating, is a happy by-product. For, a creative outcome continues to be created long after it has emerged from you. Take for example, the case of a book or painting that becomes famous long after its author has exited the scene. Or a movement or organization that goes viral and grows outside the bounds of its author's original conception or imagination. In its independent avatar, the creative outcome is being re-created or transformed into something new through every single interaction, by virtue of how it's being viewed, experienced or interpreted by audiences and connoisseurs.

All this being the case, the motivation for this practice of creativity is simply the joy of sharing – connecting with and enriching the world – an act of freely giving a gift. In his transformative book *Linchpin*, Seth Godin defines art as something freely gifted to the world. The term 'freely' doesn't qualify the economics of the interaction; to the contrary, good art, according to Godin, is unequivocally a channel of financial flow as well. What he conveys by the term 'freely' is the generosity of spirit, and the vulnerability and emotional labor required to offer one's unique gift to the world, to go every mile it takes to make it the best offer it can be, beyond the boxes and confines of the expected, the norm, the defined. Godin is speaking of surprising and delighting everyone with this kind of sky-is-the-limit effort. Whether one receives money for it or not, it is still a gift freely given because the motivation for going all out is not the money, but the Love behind the action, the joy of giving oneself fully, the delight in delighting others.

When embodying this spirit of giving and gifting one's creativity to the world, there is no room for holding back, for shying away from the limelight, for being bashful, or for playing small. As Marianne Williamson has so eloquently reminded us in *A Return to Love*, no one benefits by our playing small; rather, we liberate others to be their highest and best selves when we fully embody ours. This means standing tall to speak about one's ideas for world transformation, or singing one's heart out at every opportunity, or asking one's fear to bow out of the way when one's path-breaking blog on a taboo subject goes viral in the world, and so on.

The other beautiful quality of sharing the fruit is the depth of connection it creates with your audience. Every time someone calls or emails or walks up to me unexpectedly to tell me how a particular story or essay in one of my books has moved them or impacted their thinking, the connection made transforms both me and the other. In that moment we are connected as One by an invisible thread, spirit-to-spirit, and that single instance has the power to make my entire life worthwhile. And the other person also has a moment of vulnerability in sharing of himself, transforming him as well. Every Creativity Workshop participant who has shipped a project and has connected with audiences, reports this tremendous feeling of fulfillment from fully sharing what he or she has created.

This externally active Yang creative practice of sharing the fruit is a grateful recognition that in channeling through oneself, Spirit has given one a gift that is meant for the whole world. It is with humble gratitude for this gift, with unabashed celebration of its coming forth, and with immense generosity of spirit that one's creative outcomes must be shared with the world!

CREATIVE EXPERIMENT

Creativity Workshop participant Nimisha Ghosh Roy finds that as she practices creativity on an ongoing, consistent basis, this act of sharing the fruit gets easier. As a dancer from a young age she was always on stage performing dances that others had choreographed and taught her. As she got older and more experienced she started performing and teaching others her own choreographies. These experiences ultimately pushed her to share even more deeply of her creative self by writing for and performing in the daring project *Yoni Ki Baat* (inspired by Vagina Monologues). Soon thereafter she participated in the Creativity Workshops, and in the "totally scary, yet completely fulfilling experience" of sharing her writing in the concluding public showcase. More recently she has opened her unfolding book project *Bharati's Story* to the online community. Nimisha finds that constant practice makes it easier over time, to get over the initial hurdle, overcome the pesky lizard brain saying that it's too scary, and just get out there and share what you've created!

POSTFACE

ON SPIRIT

This is a book on the practice of creativity with the premise that creativity is a spiritual act, our very soul purpose, our true nature. So, I'd like to briefly share what I mean by spirituality, and how I've used the words spirit or soul, as well as capitalized words such as Spirit, Love, and Universe throughout the book.

I understand spirituality as *an expansion of one's awareness to be in touch with dimensions of existence beyond the material level as experienced by the mind-body complex.* Simply put, it is the 'spirit' portion of our experience – that which truly touches, moves and inspires[38] us each day!

My understanding of a higher, subtler level of existence arose from a spontaneous awakening about nine years ago, rather than from any study at all – metaphysical, spiritual, religious or otherwise. In fact, I was raised in a highly secular (and rather irreverent) environment at home as well as in the university settings my family lived in, and any appreciation of religion was strictly cultural, allegorical, moral or philosophical. If my mother dabbled in rituals it appeared entirely in passing (although a faith in something larger seemed to exist), while my father outright rejected organized religion and all ritualistic practices, along with declaring himself an atheist. Personally, while I did have an innate conception of faith, it was not as religious belief, but as an unerring knowing that Love and goodness shall always prevail.

In the context of this rather spiritually-neutral (if not void) background, it is a life crisis at the turn of thirty that became the catalyst for some powerful and transformative out-of-body experiences, which abruptly catapulted me to a higher, subtler existence, and opened me to a deep, vast, all-encompassing sense of Love and Light. Once tasted, it was

---

[38] The etymology of the word inspiration is the same as that of the word spirit!

only a matter of constant practice to intimately know this level of existence, not because I strived hard for it, but because once known it simply couldn't be unknown or forgotten! Inevitably, over time, I continued to have deeper and more vast spontaneous experiences of this higher and subtler plane. My life began to be created entirely on the basis of such higher intuition and guidance, and my previously prized intellect began to be reserved for *serving* my intuitive knowing rather than acting as the captain of my ship. In other words, my mind and body were called to *serve* my spirit, and my spirit began to commune with Spirit![39]

We know and accept on the basis of science that everything is energy. Even the densest forms of matter exhibit wave like properties. From what I sense, as human beings too, our existence extends beyond the three-dimensional material plane. Our bodies and minds (at least the brain) exist in the three-dimensional material plane, while our energetic component – a field of subtle vibrations – is what we might experience as our spirits (or souls). When we say we are *energized* or *uplifted* or *inspired* by someone's *spirited* actions, we are speaking of a palpable shift in our subtler experience that cannot be measured in material terms, even though there are accompanying material aspects such as changes in hormones, temperature or pulse rate within the body.

Our physical and mental bodies appear to be discrete and separate from one another and from the other material

---

[39] Throughout the book there are references to individual spirit and larger Spirit, but these references in dualistic terms are for exploration purposes only. My spontaneous experience is actually non-dualistic – in creative communion my spirit feels one with Spirit. So while my exposition appears to closely map with Dvaita (dualistic) Vedanta philosophy in which *Atman*, or individual spirit seeks communion with *Paramatma*, the supreme Spirit, my true inner experience is that Atman and Paramatma are really the same thing – One Atman. This understanding is more in line with Advaita (non-dualistic) Vedanta.

aspects of the Universe. In this material plane of existence, the sense of separateness is the foundation of our ego – the notion that we have individual identities, whether physical, cultural, ideological, and so on. Our spirits (that is, our energetic existences), however, connect us to each other and beyond in a seamless collective consciousness that can be instantly correlated outside the limitations of space and time. This is our higher, subtler level of existence. Crudely put, it is as if we're all computer terminals connected to and by a supercomputer! Any one terminal can generate an effect in the entire system, and conversely, all terminals draw from the larger intelligence of the system. Subtler aspects of our being such as our intentions, thoughts and feelings, conscious or unconscious, can be best understood to be in existence at the level of energy, contributing to the collective consciousness. From this understanding, one realizes that *every* thought and intention is a form of energy. It radiates into the world as karma even before any physical action is taken!

It also follows that at the higher, subtler level of existence, we are One, united with each other and with Spirit. So, when I use the term Spirit, I refer to the collective, synergistic energy that is much, much larger than the sum of its parts. This is an all-knowing, all-pervasive, omnipresent, infinite, unknowable Universal Being, and a quantum field of limitless possibility within which material occurrences come into being by intention. And, the essential quality of Spirit is Love and only Love (while all fear is an illusion in the material plane). The capitalized word Love, therefore, is used to represent the essence, the nature, and the creative power of Spirit, (while love with a little 'l' is the often fleeting feeling-state that we experience in the material plane of our existence). I sometimes use the word Universe interchangeably with Spirit, but it does mean something slightly different to me – the Universe is Spirit's reflection (and creation) in material and energetic (and other unknown) dimensions. So also, our personal realities are simply a reflection (and creation) of our individual spirit consciousness.

The presence of separateness – ego – is critical in the material plane of existence, because it is what allows us to stand back and observe 'the other.' It is with such perspective that we are able to use the material plane of existence as a playground, stage or construction site to remember and realize our spirit existence, which is only temporarily forgotten when we come into body. This is why a spiritual awakening is only a remembering (or as I like to put it, a re-membering, that is, a re-instilling of awareness in our 'members,' our bodies), always instantly available. So, paradoxically, our ego-existences are the very vehicles for us to know Truth and return home to Oneness, to Spirit! This is why intimate and sexual relationship, when based at the level of soul, is the ultimate site for spiritual awakening. By seeing ourselves mirrored in the apparent 'other' we experience and realize a seamless, profound Oneness. This sacred union of spirit with spirit then facilitates our ultimate union with Spirit.

All my ongoing insights as I am describing them here arise spontaneously from within my inner experiences, like direct 'downloads' from Spirit! I experience them as sudden inner knowing, as if I've always known them (even though I recall not knowing the previous day), and sometimes they arrive as explicit phrases, messages and visions. Experientially, they feel like remembering what I've always known and had merely forgotten, just like I've described in the previous paragraph. These insights are often miraculously and instantaneously corroborated by writings of spiritual masters; I seem to always synchronously find the exact book or audio talk or video that is necessary to expand upon or explain what I've *just* spontaneously seen in the vision of my own third eye!

Because my understanding of spirituality springs from an ongoing awakening (or remembering) experience, it is not associated with any religion. And because it is so deeply founded in Love, in which I experience human and divine Love as One, I find it easiest to associate myself with Sufism, or more generally, all mystic traditions. When I make references to religious writings from Vedanta, the Bhagavad Gita and the Bible, it is because I find resonance between these and the insights I have personally cognized through deepening spiritual experience. I sometimes also quote others, who may use the term 'God,' when I find that their essential point resonates with what I have self-cognized and am trying to convey in context, and also when I have a strong sense that their use of 'God' closely matches my use of 'Spirit.'

In practice, spirituality translates to a way of living in which one's awareness is expanded enough to be connected with one's higher and subtler level of existence, enabling a connection with one's soul purpose, with the larger Spirit, and with its essential nature of Love (or at least glimpses thereof). A spiritual existence is therefore one in which I understand that the true me *is* spirit (and via communion, Spirit!), and that the body-mind-ego complex occupying the material world is a temporary tool for self-reflection and self-expression, and ultimately, to remember Truth and return home to Oneness. Reiterating French philosopher Pierre Telhard de Chardin's oft-quoted insight,

"We are not human beings having a spiritual experience, we are spiritual beings having a human experience."

The higher, subtler level of awareness automatically reveals that the purpose of spirit – like its parent Spirit – is to *create*. The material world is a beautiful playground for such creation and self-reflection. Creativity, then, is the natural and inevitable expression of one's very existence!

REFERENCES
AND
INSPIRATIONS

Dancing About Architecture: A Little Book of Creativity, Phil Beadle, 2011

Creativity Workout: 62 Exercises to Unlock your Most Creative Ideas, Edward De Bono, 2008

I and Thou, Martin Buber, translated by Ronald Gregor Smith, 2000

Rules of the Red Rubber Ball, Kevin Carroll, 2004

Spiritual Solutions: Answers to Life's Greatest Challenges, Deepak Chopra, 2012

The Phenomenon of Man, Pierre Telhard de Chardin, 2008

Creativity: Flow and the Psychology of Discovery and Invention, Mihaly Csikszentmihalyi, 1996

Life is a Verb, Patti Digh, 2008

Creativity: Where the Divine and the Human Meet, Matthew Fox, 2002

The Mesh: Why the Future of Business is Sharing, Lisa Gansky, 2010

The Icarus Deception: How High Will You Fly?, Seth Godin, 2012

Poke the Box, Seth Godin, 2011

Linchpin: Are You Indispensable?, Seth Godin, 2010

Tribes: We Need You to Lead Us, Seth Godin, 2008

The Dip: A Little Book That Teaches You When to Quit (and When to Stick), Seth Godin, 2007

Science and the Indian Tradition: When Einstein Met Tagore, David L. Gosling, 2007

Made to Stick: Why Some Ideas Survive and Others Die, Chip Heath and Dan Heath, 2007

Power vs. Force (Revised Edition), David R. Hawkins, 2012

Synchronicity: The Inner Path of Leadership, Joseph Jaworski and Peter M. Senge, 2011

Source: The Inner Path of Knowledge Creation, Joseph Jaworski, 2012

Steal Like an Artist, Austin Kleon, 2012

Mastermind: How To Think Like Sherlock Holmes, Maria Konnikova, 2013

Evil Plans: Having Fun on the Road to World Domination, Hugh MacLeod, 2011

Ignore Everybody: and 39 Other Keys to Creativity, Hugh MacLeod, 2009

The Opposable Mind: How Successful Leaders Win Through Integrative Thinking, Roger Martin, 2007

Imagine: How Creativity Works, Jonah Lehrer, 2012

The Art of Uncertainty: How to Live in the Mystery of Life, Dennis Merritt Jones, 2011

Cracking Creativity: The Secrets of Creative Genius, Michael Michalko, 2001

Wired to Care: How Companies Prosper When They Create Widespread Empathy, Dev Patnaik with Peter Mortensen, 2009

Finding the Sweet Spot: The Natural Entrepreneur's Guide to Responsible, Sustainable, Joyful Work, Dave Pollard, 2008

Do the Work, Steven Pressfield, 2011

The War of Art: Break Through the Blocks and Win Your Inner Creative Battles, Steven Pressfield, 2002

The Element: How Finding Your Passion Changes Everything, Sir Ken Robinson, 2009

Love is the Killer App: How to Win Business and Influence Friends, Tim Sanders, 2003

How to Be an Explorer of the World, Keri Smith, 2008

The Creative Habit: Learn to Use it For Life, Twyla Tharp, 2003

Change the Way You See Everything, Kathryn D. Cramer and Hank Wasiak, 2006

A Return to Love, Marianne Williamson, 1996

The Law of Divine Compensation, Marianne Williamson, 2012

The Art of Possibility, Benjamin Zander and Rosamund Stone Zander, 2000

GRATITUDE

This book represents a culmination of insights from practicing creativity through the expression of my gifts since I was a little girl, and then, making an unexpected leap in understanding due to a spiritual awakening that began about nine years ago. So, I express my heartfelt thanks to every caregiver, teacher, friend, and collaborator I've ever had.

I thank my parents, Ranu and Sushanta Dattagupta for this precious life, and for recognizing and nurturing my creativity from a very young age. My deep relationship with my sister in both blood and spirit, Sharmishtha Dattagupta, has contributed greatly to my spiritual insight. I am deeply grateful to my parents, sister, and entire extended family for continuously believing in me and my path, and for their unconditional Love, support and blessings.

I thank Amrita Madan and Rupamanjari Ghosh for a lifetime of co-creativity, friendship, understanding, Love and family.

I thank my esteemed Gurus, Pandita Tripti Mukherjee and Sangeet Martand Pandit Jasraj, for showing me Light and Love through divine music and so much more. I also thank all those who entrust their musical journeys to me, for when I sing to guide them is when I truly learn.

I thank Andrew McCune for rekindling my creativity, purpose, heart and life when I thought they (and I) were dead. I thank Robb Hamilton and Rachael Victoria, and their boys Macky and Grady, for being my family when I was entirely lost. I thank Anya Woestwin and David Gibson for creating spaces for deep healing. I thank Sabina Ansari, Manoj Biswas, Priyam Das, Bidisha Ghosh, Srivani Jade, Arijit Mahanalabis, Mausam, Checha Sokolovic, and Tully Wehr for their friendships and shared creative / spiritual paths that have made me what I am today. And I thank Scott Francis, Robert Mankin, and Jonathan Ward for transformative creative collaborations that brought the best out of me, and showed me how anything is possible when we act in authentic, synergistic co-creation.

I thank Jason Week for his kind and loving friendship, and his tangible, steadfast, and unconditional support through the last several years of metamorphosis, always unselfishly reminding me, "You've got to be you."

I thank Farah Abdul, Manoj and Rita Biswas, Devasmita Chakraverty, Pallavi Garg, Sudha Nandagopal, Runika Nandakumar, Paj Nandi, Prasun and Sudeshna Raha, and Archana Verma for their deep friendship and consistent, caring support over the last year as this book came through.

I thank Indira and EGP Haran for showing up miraculously like godparents, instantly showering me with a lifetime's worth of understanding, blessings and Love, renewing and deepening my faith in my chosen path.

I thank intuitive healer, spiritual teacher and visionary, Jenna Forrest, for guiding me deeply on the nature of soul relationships, and their higher purpose in serving creativity and the healing of humanity. Specifically for this book, her teachings on the importance of balancing the feminine and masculine energies for true harmony in this world, inspired me to explore creative principles in terms of Yin and Yang, and develop the entire second half of the book along those lines.

I thank Helen Lowe of Catalytica for an important summer of collaboration on creativity and innovation, leading to the co-creation of a large-format Creativity Workshop, the process of which clarified my thinking in writing this book.

I thank my friend and co-creative Ashok Das for drawing the brilliant cover illustration, capturing with telepathic efficiency and in one fell swoop, the essence of this book. And I thank my friend and co-creative Pallavi Garg for letting me introduce the book's premise with her beautifully resonant poem.

I'm very grateful to all the creatives who trust me to coach and witness them as they unlock their full creative potential. It is for them that this book *had* to be. Over and above, I thank Pallavi Garg, Sheeba Marie Jacob, Kamal Janardhan, Rashmi Thirtha Jyoti, Sudha Nandagopal, Nimisha Ghosh Roy, Arathi Srikantaiah, and Dharini Vasudevan for sharing their creative experiments for publication in this book.

Shirin Subhani, my beloved friend and partner in *Flying Chickadee*, makes anything and everything possible! As with all my other works and initiatives, Shirin has co-created with me, exploring possibility and providing inspiration, ideas, and all manner of support, besides reviewing and editing the book and developing the *Reflections* inserts in the first two chapters. (All failings in the book are, of course, solely mine.) Most importantly, Shirin has courageously taken the leap of faith with me into the practice of creativity, and has always generously given her Love. I also thank Shirin's boys Aadit and Arnav for being our teachers, and her husband Naveen Valluri for his heartfelt support in all our shared endeavors.

Murali Haran also makes anything and everything possible! By simply being who he is, he has inspired and deepened my Love, creative power, and understanding of self and Spirit, in the most profound and compelling way yet. Serving as *saathi* and *saarathi*,[40] whether in-person or from a distance, his gentle, unselfconscious and neutral witnessing on the one hand, and his insightful and deep but lighthearted soul-mirroring on the other, have summoned the highest and best of me to write this book. (He has no direct association with or responsibility for the book's contents or philosophy.) I am, of course, still sculpting away the debris to reveal the best

---

[40] Translate from Hindi roughly as "friend" and "guide."

of me. To that end, this book has written me, rather than the other way around!

No work is complete without acknowledging the divine feline presence in my life. My cuddly thanks go to Lailah and Sid for reminding me of the little things that matter most, every single day.

Most of all I am eternally grateful to Spirit for gracing me with Presence and channeling through me as creative expression. It is a profoundly humbling and awe-inspiring experience and I ask to serve in this way forever.

Made in the USA
Charleston, SC
28 March 2013